GENESIS AS HISTORY:

BIBLICAL AND SCIENTIFIC EVIDENCE THAT GENESIS PRESENTS THE TRUTH ABOUT EARTH'S HISTORY

Daniel A. Biddle, Ph.D.

GENESIS
apologetics

www.genesisapologetics.com: A 501(c)(3) ministry equipping youth pastors, parents, and students with Biblical answers for evolutionary teaching in public schools.

GENESIS AS HISTORY: BIBLICAL AND SCIENTIFIC
EVIDENCE THAT GENESIS PRESENTS THE TRUTH
ABOUT EARTH'S HISTORY
by Daniel A. Biddle, Ph.D.
Printed in the United States of America

ISBN-13: 978-1542970211

ISBN-10: 1542970210

Download our FREE Mobile App with Creation-Evolution Videos!

Dedication

To my wife, Jenny, who supports me in this work. To my children Makaela, Alyssa, Matthew, and Amanda, and to your children and your children's children for a hundred generations—this book is for all of you.

We would like to acknowledge Answers in Genesis (*www.answersingenesis.org*), the Institute for Creation Research (*www.icr.org*), and Creation Ministries International (*www.creation.com*). Much of the content herein has been drawn from (and is meant to be in alignment with) these Biblical Creation ministries.

"Guard what has been entrusted to you, avoiding worldly and empty chatter and the opposing arguments of what is falsely called 'knowledge'—which some have professed and thus gone astray from the faith. Grace be with you."
—1 Tim. 6:20–21

"This is the Lord's doing; it is marvelous in our eyes."
—Psalm 118:23

Contents

About the Author

Dr. Daniel A. Biddle is president of Genesis Apologetics, Inc. a 501(C)(3) organization dedicated to equipping youth pastors, parents, and students with Biblical answers for evolutionary teaching in public schools. Daniel has trained thousands of students in Biblical Creation and evolution and is the author of several Creation-related publications. Daniel also serves as the Vice Chairman of the Board of The International Association for Creation, a non-profit ministry serving to unify the Biblical Creation movement. Daniel's experience and qualification in the secular realm includes a Ph.D. in Organizational Psychology from Alliant University in San Francisco, California, an M.A. in Organizational Psychology from Alliant, and a B.S. in Organizational Behavior from the University of San Francisco. Daniel has worked as an expert consultant and/or witness in over 100 state and federal cases in the areas of research methodologies and analysis.

About Genesis Apologetics

Genesis Apologetics is a non-profit 501(C)(3) ministry that equips Christian students and their parents with faith-building materials that reaffirm a Biblical Creation worldview. We are committed to providing Christian families with Biblically- and scientifically-based answers to the evolutionary theory that many children are taught in public schools. Our doctrinal position on Creation aligns with Answers in Genesis and the Institute for Creation Research (ICR), two of the largest Creation Apologetic Ministries in the U.S.

Readers are encouraged to download our free Mobile App from the iTunes or Google Play stores and view our free training resources at *www.debunkevolution.com, www.genesisapologetics.com* and our YouTube Channel (Channel Name: Genesis Apologetics).

Preface

Believing and Doing

People tend to act much differently when they *really* believe something. An Air Force pilot only uses full thrusters when flying a jet off an aircraft carrier when they *really* believe their jet will take off before the end of the short runway. A soldier wears armor over his vital areas before close quarter combat because he really believes his opponent can harm him. An expert witness will testify in a court case when she believes she has a solid command of the facts in the case.

This close connection between belief and actions also applies to spiritual matters. Christians begin to live under the authority of the Bible when they believe it's actually true—both theologically *and* historically. A college student who isn't sure that the Bible is a divinely-inspired book—one that includes an accurate account of Earth history—will be less likely to trust its moral warnings when it comes to making right or wrong choices.

How I Began to Believe

Personally, my Christian life totally changed after I understood that Genesis includes *real history*. Without even knowing it, I used to have a hidden, dark fog of doubt in my mind. Doubt kept my heart from having full and complete faith in Christ and the Bible that tells us all about Him. Even though I had received Christ at an early age (11) and have been walking with him since age 17, for years I was not really sure where to fit Biblical history into my belief system. Don't get me wrong—even as a seminary student in my 30s, I would have told you that I believed the whole Bible, but now I see that I was unsure about the very beginning. When going through Genesis, the seminary professors did a good job of explaining how the original language of Genesis 1 and connecting genealogies of Genesis 5 clearly led to a "young earth" (fitting inside 10,000 years). However, they were also quick to point out that secular science seemed to have a lock-tight case of millions of years. They left it up to us students to figure out our own answers, but provided no tools.

After years of living with this unresolved tension, I heard a talk on dinosaurs and Noah's Flood—a talk that explored evidence that seemed to back a straight-forward reading of Genesis.

A Fascinating Research Journey

That began a season of intense research on the two topics of Noah's Flood and dinosaurs. Being trained as a behavioral scientist, I was familiar with the distinctions between good and bad "evidence," and I used these skills in wading my way through mounds of material covering Earth science, archeology, paleontology, Biblical interpretation, and geology.

One thing I learned through my career as a professional expert witness is that law courts maintain certain standards for admitting evidence. Evidence that comes by "hearsay" or unverifiable historic documents cannot be placed into the evidence docket in many types of cases because they cannot be *verified* and *tested*. I knew that both Biblical Creation and evolution both suffered from this limitation because we simply cannot go back thousands of years and observe the unfolding of the Creation Week described in the first chapter of Genesis. Likewise, we cannot go back to see if millions of years really happened. I knew that both views required *faith*.

Throughout this process, I learned that God wanted me to first trust completely in His Word. Only then did He lead me through the "evidence journey" that showed me that His Word was plainly written and historically true. So, for me, trust in His Word was required before the unveiling of the evidence that confirmed it to be true.

The other major lesson that I learned through this research journey was how hard the world fights against God's truth. Western culture powerfully promotes millions of years and evolution at every turn. State parks, movies, television, museums, children's books, public school curricula—everywhere I turned, my "newly opened eyes" saw the lie of evolution on its imaginary foundation of deep time.

What do you believe about Genesis? Does your story sound like mine? Would you consider evidence that fits the unpopular idea that Genesis conveys history and not mere fairy tales?

What to Expect in This Book

To start this journey through the convincing evidence that supports Biblical Creation, the first chapter will review the reasons we can trust that the Bible was divinely inspired and reliably recorded over the centuries. Chapter 2 covers the biblical case for recent creation using a dialogue between two Christians. Chapter 3 exposes critical flaws with radiometric dating. Chapter 4 reviews how dinosaurs fit into the biblical timeline. Chapter 5 reviews the world's idea of human evolution and shows ten evidences that show "Lucy's" ape kind did not connect to man. We conclude with Chapter 6 and a look at the reasons why theistic evolution fails to fit the Bible and can harm Christian believers.

For video-based training on the same topics covered by this book, please download our free Mobile App from the iTunes or Google Play stores and view our free training resources at *www.debunkevolution.com,* *www.genesisapologetics.com* and our YouTube Channel (Channel Name: Genesis Apologetics).

Introduction: A Special Creation

When it comes to interpreting the Scriptures, some Bible scholars offer a foundational rule: "Let Scripture interpret Scripture." This certainly applies when it comes to trying to understand something as incomprehensible as the creation of the world and everything in it. While the first chapter of Genesis certainly provides more details about Creation than any other Bible passage, some Scriptures offer insight into how God created.

For example, Hebrews 11:3 states: "By *faith* we understand that the worlds were *framed by the word of God*, so that the things which are seen were not made of things which are visible." When speaking about the angels, sun, moon, and stars, Psalm 148:5 declares "He *commanded* and they were created." Psalm 33:8–9 adds: "Let all the earth fear the Lord; Let all the inhabitants of the world stand in awe of Him. For *He spoke*, and it was done; He *commanded*, and it stood fast."

These verses are clear: God created everything from nothing, and He did it by *speaking; by commanding*. The universe was not made from pre-existing materials of any kind. This rules out the idea of theistic evolution, as we'll see in the chapter on that subject. Only an all-powerful God can command Creation into existence, and this is exactly how the Bible said He did it! Further, all of Creation was finished after Creation Week: "And yet his works have been *finished* since the creation of the world" (Hebrews 4:3).

All three persons of the Trinity were involved in the Creation process. The Holy Spirit was "hovering over the waters" (Genesis 1:2) and it was by Jesus that "all things were created that are in heaven and that are on earth, visible and invisible, whether thrones or dominions or principalities or powers." John 1:3 states that "All things were made through Him [Jesus], and without Him [Jesus] nothing was made that was made." Please keep this in mind as a possibility when reading the rest of this book…

Chapter 1: The Bible
How Do We Know the Bible Is Reliable and Was Translated Accurately over the Centuries?

Let's start this chapter by allowing the Bible to speak for itself. The Bible claims to be unlike any other book on the planet. Let's look at a few key passages to this effect:

- 2 Timothy 3:16–17: All Scripture is given by inspiration of God, and is profitable for doctrine, for reproof, for correction, for instruction in righteousness, that the man of God may be complete, thoroughly equipped for every good work.
- 2 Peter 1:20–21: Knowing this first, that no prophecy of Scripture is of any private interpretation, for prophecy never came by the will of man, but holy men of God spoke as they were moved by the Holy Spirit.

In addition to these key verses, the Bible is filled with passages that describe God's Word to be consistently true, unchanging, perfect, permanent, and even honored by God along with His own name.[1] But the Bible goes even further.

Did you know that the Bible offers real, tangible life benefits for those who obey it? No, this isn't "prosperity" teaching. There are some Bible passages that are very clear regarding the rewards for those who take it seriously.

For example, Psalm 19:11 states: "Moreover by them [God's collective Word] your servant is warned, and *in keeping them there is great reward*" (emphasis added). This verse is speaking of a reward for obedience that will be received here and now. The words "in" and "is" mean that great reward follows the actual process of doing God's will and keeping His commandments, like the commandment to trust Him.[2]

The words of Jesus are of course Scripture. Listen to what He says about those who keep His Word:

Therefore, whoever hears these sayings of Mine, and does them, I will liken him to a wise man who built his house on the rock: and the rain descended, the floods came, and the winds blew and beat on that house; and it did not fall, for it was founded on the rock. But everyone who hears these sayings of Mine, and does not do them, will be like a foolish man who built his house on the sand: and the rain descended, the floods came, and the winds blew and beat on that house; and it fell. And great was its fall. (Matthew 7:24–27)

Jesus is clear that there are rewards ahead for those who live under His Word. By first believing His Word—including the beginning—and then living under the authority of Scripture, we allow the Lord to build our lives on His foundation, the strongest foundation there is. But there are more reasons than just these promises to trust what the Bible says.

How Was the Bible Assembled?

So many people ask: Who wrote the Bible? How was the Bible put together? How do we know the stories in the Bible actually happened? How do we know that it has been accurately transmitted over the years? These are all fair questions. To start answering some of these questions, we will begin by looking at the big picture, then follow with a closer look.

The big picture begins with the Bible's 66 books (39 books in the Old Testament and 27 books in the New Testament) that were written by over 40 different authors from various walks of life, including scholars, kings, priests, shepherds, farmers, physicians, tent-makers, fishermen, and philosophers. The first books of the Bible were compiled around 1450 BC and the last books before AD 90—a timespan of about 1,500 years. It was written in three languages: Hebrew, Aramaic, and Greek. The most important characteristic of the

15

Bible—and one that makes it different than any other book ever published—is that it is inspired by God (2 Timothy 3:16–17 and 2 Peter 1:19–21).

Despite such a diverse background, the Bible is unlike any other book written in history in its historical accuracy, agreement with demonstrable science and archaeology, and consistency—both internally and externally. The Bible has been translated into over 2,000 languages and ranks highest among the most widely printed and studied books in the world.

Let's take a closer look into how the Bible was put together. The first 39 books of the Bible (the Old Testament) were solidified and used authoritatively in its complete form by the Hebrews well before the time of Christ. The books of the New Testament were written between about AD 40 and AD 90 and were formally "canonized" into the set of 27 books we have today sometime before the year AD 375 The word "canon" comes from the Greek word *kanon*, which means "measuring rod." This word was used by those who officially verified an assembled set of 27 books because they stood up to the measuring tests of "divine inspiration and authority."

What led to this final "canonization" process? Theology and history books have thousands of pages on this topic. So, we'll consider just a few highlights between the time the New Testament was *inspired* by God through original manuscripts men wrote and *assembled* into the "final canon":[3]

- Paul regarded Luke's writings to be as authoritative as the Old Testament (1 Timothy 5:18; see also Deuteronomy 25:4 and Luke 10:7).
- Peter recognized Paul's writings as Scripture (2 Peter 3:15–16).
- Some of the books of the New Testament were being circulated among the churches (Colossians 4:16; 1 Thessalonians 5:27).
- Clement of Rome mentioned at least eight New Testament books (AD 95).

- The writings of Ignatius of Antioch acknowledged about seven New Testament books (AD 115).
- The writings of Polycarp, a disciple of John the Apostle, acknowledged 15 of the books (AD 108). Later, Irenaeus mentioned 21 New Testament books (AD 185).
- Hippolytus of Rome recognized 22 of them (AD 170–235).

Before the final set of 27 books was formally recognized, an earlier "canon" was compiled in AD 170. This Canon, called the Muratorian Canon, included all the New Testament books except Hebrews, James, and 3 John. These three books were already God-inspired even though the writer of the Muratorian Canon may not have recognized them as so. In AD 363, the Council of Laodicea stated that only the Old Testament and the 27 books of the New Testament were to be read in the churches. The Council of Hippo (AD 393) and the Council of Carthage (AD 397) also affirmed the same 27 books as authoritative.

We owe these ancient councilmen. They sifted through false gospels and other writings that early deceivers claimed were God-inspired so that later generations of Christians could trust, study, know, teach, and believe in the Scriptures. Some of the features they recognized in the canon included:

- Did the text describe mythological or pointless miracles, or genuine miracles which always accompanied and authorized a message—the Gospel.
- Did the people who lived through the events that the text describes reject those texts as being false, or accept them as having occurred as described?
- Did the text contain any logical or biblical contradictions? If so, it must not have come from the same Divine co-author, who is not a God of confusion, but of order—and who is passionate about clearly revealing who He is to as many as will listen; and

- Was the text written by an apostle or one authorized by an apostle?

After this "canonization" period, a definitive version of the Bible was recorded in Greek, called the *Codex Vaticanus* in about AD 350. The classic King James version, as well as the New King James, relied on a different family of manuscripts often called the *Textus Receptus*. The Codex is one of the oldest extant manuscripts of the Greek Bible (Old and New Testament), and has been kept in the Vatican Library since the 15th century. Another ancient Bible is the *Aleppo Codex*, which is a medieval bound manuscript of the Hebrew Bible written around AD 930. Comparing these early versions with each other shows very few copyist errors occurred. And of those few, none change any central teaching.

The first English translation of the Bible was made in AD 1382 by John Wycliffe and was the first book ever mass-produced on the printing press in AD 1454 by Johannes Gutenberg.[4]

Given this brief history, let's put the Bible through some tests that historians use when analyzing the historical accuracy and reliability of ancient manuscripts. First, let's evaluate whether *what we have today matches what was written originally*. In the Bible's case, this was about 2,000 years ago and earlier. Second: *Do the recorded events describe true events*? Let's see how the Bible holds up to each of these important questions.

Does Today's Bible Match the Original?

One of the primary ways to answer this important question is to look at the *time gap* between the original writing (called the *autograph*) and the copies that still exist today. As a general rule, the closer the copy is to the original, the greater the accuracy and reliability. Ancient manuscripts (hand-written copies) of books like the Bible were written on fragile material such as papyrus, which is a thin paper-like material made from papyrus plants. Because papyrus eventually decays or gets worn out, ancient writers would continually make new copies using this material and others.[5]

Dating these ancient texts is done by a variety of methods, such as analyzing the material on which it was written, letter size and form, punctuation, text divisions, ornamentation, the color of the ink, and the texture and color of the parchment.[6] Table 1 shows the results of this "test of time" for the Biblical New Testament compared to several other historical documents.

Table 1. How the New Testament Compares to Other Ancient Manuscript Writings.[7]

Author/Work	Date Written	Earliest Copies	Time Gap	Num. Copies
Homer (Iliad)	800 BC	400 BC	400 yrs.	643
Herodotus (History)	480–425 BC	AD 900	1,350 yrs.	8
Thucydides (History)	460–400 BC	AD 900	1,300 yrs.	8
Plato	400 BC	AD 900	1,300 yrs.	7
Demosthenes	300 BC	AD 1100	1,400 yrs.	200
Caesar (Gallic Wars)	100–44 BC	AD 900	1,000 yrs.	10
Tacitus (Annals)	AD 100	AD 1100	1,000 yrs.	20
Pliny (Natural) Secundus (History)	AD 61–113	AD 850	750 yrs.	7
New Testament (Fragment)	AD 50–100	AD 114	50 yrs.	5,366
New Testament (Books)		AD 200	100 yrs.	
New Testament (Most Content)		AD 250	150 yrs.	
New Testament (Complete)		AD 325	225 yrs.	

Table 1 reveals two important facts. First, the New Testament has many more manuscript copies compared to several other famous pieces of literature (5,366 compared to only hundreds for other famous texts). Second, it reveals that the time span between the original and these copies is closer than almost any other work compared!

Answering the important question, *"Does the Bible we have today match what was written originally?"* requires evaluating the *number of manuscript copies* that were made of the original. Generally speaking, the greater number of copies of the original available, the easier it is to reproduce the original. Taking the 5,366 copies of the New Testament and adding the copies from other languages (such as Latin, Ethiopic, and Slavic) results in more than 25,000 total manuscripts that pre-date the printing press in the 15th century! By comparison, the runner-up historical text (Homer's Iliad) has only 643.[8]

With this, the New Testament clearly passes both the *time gap* and the *number of manuscript copies* tests. And if the New Testament doesn't pass this test, one must certainly disregard most other historical texts as inaccurate and/or unreliable!

There is more.

Have you ever had a computer crash, resulting in a total loss of all your data? I have—it's definitely not fun! One of the most difficult challenges about computer crashes is losing the *original copies* of your important homework assignments or work reports. However, when I've experienced these situations, I'm usually able to completely reconstruct all my important "final versions" through my *email files* because I sent copies of the final versions to friends or clients. This is the same situation with the original Bible documents and the letter exchanges between the Church Fathers (the early leaders of the church)— we can completely reconstruct over 99% of the original Bible (New Testament) from just their letters!

Even if all the copies of the Bible from AD 300 to today were destroyed, the complete New Testament (except for only 11 verses)[9] could be reconstructed using only quotations by the

Early Church Fathers in the first few hundred years after Christ! This is because the Church Fathers frequently quoted large sections of Scripture in their letters to each other. In addition, if these Church Fathers quoted from the entire New Testament, then the New Testament had to have been widely circulating before this time—long enough to be regarded as reliable by the early church. This shows that the entire New Testament was already assembled and considered reliable within 50 years from the disciples.[10]

Is What Was Written in the Bible True?

Three of the four Gospels, books that include the narrative of Jesus' life, were written by *direct eye witnesses* of the events in Jesus' life: Matthew, Mark, and John. The fourth Gospel was written by Luke for Theophilus, a high-ranking official at the time.[11] Luke wrote: "Many have undertaken to draw up an account of the things that have been fulfilled among us, *just as they were handed down to us by those who from the first were eyewitnesses and servants of the word*" (Luke 1:1–2, emphasis added). Luke continues to state that he carefully vetted his account of Jesus' life and ministry: "With this in mind, since I myself have carefully investigated everything from the beginning, I too decided to write an orderly account for you, most excellent Theophilus, so that you may know the certainty of the things you have been taught" (Luke 1:3–4). Additional examples of this careful research and transcription include:

- 1 John 1:3: We proclaim to you what we have seen and heard, so that you also may have fellowship with us. And our fellowship is with the Father and with his Son, Jesus Christ.
- 2 Peter 1:16: For we did not follow cleverly devised stories when we told you about the coming of our Lord

Jesus Christ in power, but we were eyewitnesses of his majesty.

- John 20:30–31: Jesus performed many other signs in the presence of his disciples, which are not recorded in this book. But these are written that you may believe that Jesus is the Messiah, the Son of God, and that by believing you may have life in his name.

In addition, several of the writers of the New Testament did their writing and speaking among people who were present during the events of Jesus's life. For example, in Acts 2:22, Peter stated while under interrogation, "Fellow Israelites, listen to this: Jesus of Nazareth was a man accredited by God to you by miracles, wonders and signs, which *God did among you through him, as you yourselves know*" (emphasis added). Paul used this reference to his audience's common knowledge of Christ when he defended himself against Festus: "What I am saying is true and reasonable. *The king is familiar with these things*, and I can speak freely to him. I am convinced that none of this has escaped his notice, because it was not done in a corner" (Acts 26:25–26, emphasis added).

Furthermore, most of the writings of the New Testament were written during a time when the community knew about Jesus, Jesus' followers, or knew of people who did. "For what I received I passed on to you as of first importance: that Christ died for our sins according to the Scriptures, that he was buried, that he was raised on the third day according to the Scriptures, and that he appeared to Cephas, and then to the Twelve. After that, he appeared to more than five hundred of the brothers and sisters at the same time, most of whom are still living, though some have fallen asleep" (1 Corinthians 15:3–6, emphasis added).

Finally, consider the fact that 11 of the 12 disciples died terrible deaths—being killed for their unchanging testimony of who Christ was, and of His resurrection.[12] They were so sure that Christ was who He claimed to be that they signed their testimony with their own blood!

Isaiah 53 and the Dead Sea Scrolls

In 1947, shepherds chasing a lost sheep in the caves above the Qumran Valley northwest of the Dead Sea made one of the most significant archaeological discoveries of our time— the Dead Sea Scrolls. Over 900 scrolls were found in numerous clay jars, and 200 of the scrolls include numerous sections and fragments of every book in the Old Testament except the book of Esther. Though few of its scholars dare admit it, they even contain fragments of several New Testament books.[13]

One of the most significant scrolls is called the "Great Isaiah Scroll," which includes the same Book of Isaiah that we have today in modern bibles, but dates to 125 BC.[14] The Great Isaiah Scroll is significant for two reasons. First, it was written before the Lord Jesus Christ was yet born, and it includes a chapter (Chapter 53) which includes specific and clear prophecies about the torture, death, burial, and resurrection of Christ. Second, its discovery now allows us to test three versions of the Bible representing different time periods: Pre-Christ Dead Sea Scroll, AD 930, and today. We can even compare how the English translation of this important text survived or changed through the years!

Table 2 provides a word-by-word comparison of these three versions so you can see for yourself how reliable the transmission process has been through the millennia:

Table 2. Comparison of Isaiah 53 between the Dead Sea Scrolls, the Aleppo Codex, and the Modern Bible.[15]

Verse	Dead Sea "Great Isaiah" Scroll (125 BC)	Aleppo Codex (AD 930)	Modern Translation (NIV)
1	Who has believed our report and the arm of YHWH [(1)] to whom has it been revealed?	Who would have believed our report? And to whom hath the arm of the LORD been revealed?	Who has believed our message and to whom has the arm of the LORD been revealed?
2	And he shall come up like a suckling before us and as a root from dry ground there is no form to him and no beauty to him and in his being seen and there is no appearance that we should desire him.	For he shot up right forth as a sapling, and as a root out of a dry ground; he had no form nor comeliness that we should look upon him, nor beauty that we should delight in him.	He grew up before him like a tender shoot, and like a root out of dry ground. He had no beauty or majesty to attract us to him, nothing in his appearance that we should desire him.
3	He is despised and rejected of men, a man of sorrows and knowing grief and as though hiding faces from him he was despised and we did not esteem him.	He was despised, and forsaken of men, a man of pains, and acquainted with disease, and as one from whom men hide their face: he was despised, and we esteemed him not.	He was despised and rejected by men, a man of sorrows, and familiar with suffering. Like one from whom men hide their faces he was despised, and we esteemed him not.
4	Surely our griefs he is bearing and our sorrows he carried them and we esteemed him beaten and struck by God and afflicted.	Surely our diseases he did bear, and our pains he carried; whereas we did esteem him stricken, smitten of God, and afflicted.	Surely he took up our infirmities and carried our sorrows, yet we considered him stricken by God, smitten by him, and afflicted.
5	and he is wounded for our transgressions, and crushed for our iniquities, the correction of our peace was upon him and by his wounds he has healed us.[(2)]	But he was wounded because of our transgressions, he was crushed because of our iniquities: the chastisement of our welfare was upon him, and with his stripes we were healed.	But he was pierced for our transgressions, he was crushed for our iniquities; the punishment that brought us peace was upon him, and by his wounds we are healed.
6	All of us like sheep have wandered each man to his own way we have turned and YHWH has caused to light on him the iniquity of all of us.	All we like sheep did go astray, we turned every one to his own way; and the LORD hath made to light on him the iniquity of us all.	We all, like sheep, have gone astray, each of us has turned to his own way; and the LORD has laid on him the iniquity of us all.
7	He was oppressed and he was afflicted and he did not open his mouth, as a lamb to the slaughter he is brought and as a ewe before her shearers is made dumb he did not open his mouth.	He was oppressed, though he humbled himself and opened not his mouth; as a lamb that is led to the slaughter, and as a sheep that before her shearers is dumb; yea, he opened not his mouth.	He was oppressed and afflicted, yet he did not open his mouth; he was led like a lamb to the slaughter, and as a sheep before her shearers is silent, so he did not open his mouth.

8	From prison and from judgment he was taken and his generation who shall discuss it because he was cut off from the land of the living. Because from the transgressions of his people a wound was to him.	By oppression and judgment he was taken away, and with his generation who did reason? for he was cut off out of the land of the living, for the transgression of my people to whom the stroke was due.	By oppression and judgment he was taken away. And who can speak of his descendants? For he was cut off from the land of the living; for the transgression of my people he was stricken.
9	And they gave wicked ones to be his grave and (3) rich ones in his death although he worked no violence neither deceit in his mouth.	And they made his grave with the wicked, and with the rich his tomb; although he had done no violence, neither was any deceit in his mouth.	He was assigned a grave with the wicked, and with the rich in his death, though he had done no violence, nor was any deceit in his mouth.
10	And YHWH was pleased to crush him and He has caused him grief. If you will appoint his soul a sin offering he will see his seed and he will lengthen his days and the pleasure of YHWH in his hand will advance.	Yet it pleased the LORD to crush him by disease; to see if his soul would offer itself in restitution, that he might see his seed, prolong his days, and that the purpose of the LORD might prosper by his hand:	Yet it was the LORD's will to crush him and cause him to suffer, and though the LORD makes his life a guilt offering, he will see his offspring and prolong his days, and the will of the LORD will prosper in his hand.
11	Of the toil of his soul he shall see {+light+} and he shall be satisfied and by his knowledge shall he make righteous even my righteous servant for many and their iniquities he will bear.	Of the travail of his soul he shall see to the full, even My servant, who by his knowledge did justify the Righteous One to the many, and their iniquities he did bear.	After the suffering of his soul, he will see the light [of life] and be satisfied; by his knowledge my righteous servant will justify many, and he will bear their iniquities.
12	Therefore I will apportion to him among the great ones and with the mighty ones he shall divide the spoil because he laid bare to death his soul and with the transgressors he was numbered, and he, the sins of many, he bore, and for their transgressions he entreated.	Therefore will I divide him a portion among the great, and he shall divide the spoil with the mighty; because he bared his soul unto death, and was numbered with the transgressors; yet he bore the sin of many, and made intercession for the transgressors.	Therefore I will give him a portion among the great, and he will divide the spoils with the strong, because he poured out his life unto death, and was numbered with the transgressors. For he bore the sin of many, and made intercession for the transgressors.

Notes: (1) The tetragrammaton (YHWH) is one of the names of the God of Israel used in the Hebrew Bible. (2) There is a scribal thumb print over lines 10 to 12 in the Dead Sea "Isaiah" Scroll (lines 10–12 include verses 5–7 in modern Bibles). However, while this obscures some letters, all letters are "reconstructible with certainty" (see: *http://www.ao.net/~fmoeller/qum-44.htm*); (3) a scribbled word probably the accusative sign "eth."

Table 2 shows that scribes maintained an incredibly high degree of similarity over millennia. In fact, regarding this specific chapter in Isaiah, renowned Christian philosopher and apologist Norman Geisler writes:

> Of the 166 words in Isaiah 53, there are only 17 letters in question. Ten of these letters are simply a matter of spelling, which does not affect the sense. Four more letters are minor stylistic changes, such as conjunctions. The remaining three letters comprise the word "light" which is added in verse 11, and does not affect the meaning greatly. Furthermore, this word is supported by the Septuagint and IQ Is [first cave of Qumran, Isaiah scroll]. Thus, in one chapter of 166 words, there is only one word (three letters) in question after a thousand years of transmission—and this word does not significantly change the meaning of the passage.[16]

How is this possible? How can these three different documents—being translated and transcribed over a 2,000-year timeframe—have such *incredible* similarity? One explanation is simply that God watched over the process. Practically speaking, he used many incredible scribes to do it. For example, the Talmudists (Hebrew scribes and scholars between AD 100 and AD 500) had an incredibly rigorous system for transcribing biblical scrolls. Samuel Davidson describes some of the disciplines of the Talmudists in regard to the Scriptures:[17]

> A synagogue roll must be written on the skins of clean animals, prepared for the particular use of the synagogue by a Jew. These must be fastened together with strings taken from clean animals. Every skin must contain a certain number of columns, equal throughout the entire codex. The

length of each column must not extend over less than 48 or more than 60 lines; And the breadth must consist of thirty letters. The whole copy must be first-lined; And if three words be written without a line, it is worthless. The ink should be black, neither red, green, nor any other color, and be prepared according to a definite recipe. An authentic copy must be the exemplar, from which the transcriber ought not in the least deviate. No word or letter, not even a yod, must be written from memory, the scribe not having looked at the codex before him... Between every consonant the space of a hair or thread must intervene; Between every new parashah, or section, the breadth of nine consonants; Between every book, three lines. The fifth book of Moses must terminate exactly with a line; But the rest need not do so. Besides this, the copyist must sit in full Jewish dress, wash his whole body, not begin to write the name of God with a pen newly dipped in ink, and should a king address him while writing that name, he must take no notice of him.

Why is Isaiah 53 so important to Christians? It's important because Isaiah 53 includes at least 12 highly specific prophecies regarding the life, death, and resurrection of Christ. The details in this chapter would not be nearly as important if they were written after Christ's birth, but the fact that we can confirm that the chapter was in fact written before Christ proves beyond reasonable doubt both the accuracy and Divine authorship of the Bible. Consider these 12 prophecies, originally written by Isaiah about 700 years before Christ was even born, alongside references of their New Testament fulfillments:

1. He would not be widely believed (John 1:10–12).
2. He would not have the look of Majesty (Luke 2:7).
3. He would be despised and suffer (Matthew 26:67–68; 27:39–43).
4. He would be concerned about health needs (Matthew 8:17) and would die for our sins (1 Peter 2:24).
5. His pain/punishment would be for us (Matthew 28:20; Romans 4:25).
6. He would not respond to charges (Matthew 26:63).
7. He was to be oppressed and killed (Matthew 26:65–68).
8. He was associated with criminals during life and at death (Matthew 27:38, 27:57–60).
9. He would be buried in a rich man's tomb (Isaiah 53:9).
10. He would be crushed, suffer, and die, yet live (Luke 23:44–48, 24:36–44).
11. He would bear our sins (1 Peter 2:24).
12. He would have a portion with the great (Philippians 2:8–11).

Now that we have the Dead Sea Scrolls, we can confirm that these prophecies were *written before Christ even walked the earth*! How could anyone fulfill each of these prophecies, many of which happened after Christ's death and were clearly out of His control (i.e., if he wasn't God)? Finally, consider these prophecies about Christ that were all penned before He was born, and their fulfillments:[18]

Table 3. Forty three (43) Prophecies Fulfilled by Jesus.

Prophecies About Jesus	Old Test. Scripture	New Testament Fulfillment
Messiah would be born in Bethlehem.	Micah 5:2	Matthew 2:1; Luke 2:4–6
Messiah would be born of a virgin.	Isaiah 7:14	Matthew 1:22–23; Luke 1:26–31
Messiah would come from the line of Abraham.	Genesis 12:3, 22:18	Matthew 1:1; Romans 9:5
Messiah would be a descendant of Isaac.	Genesis 17:19, 21:12	Luke 3:34
Messiah would be a descendant of Jacob.	Numbers 24:17	Matthew 1:2
Messiah would come from the tribe of Judah.	Genesis 49:10	Luke 3:33; Hebrews 7:14
Messiah would be heir to King David's throne.	2 Sam. 7:12-13; Isa. 9:7	Luke 1:32–33; Romans 1:3
Messiah's throne will be anointed and eternal.	Ps. 45:6–7; Daniel 2:44	Luke 1:33; Hebrews 1:8–12
Messiah would be called Immanuel.	Isaiah 7:14	Matthew 1:23
Messiah would spend a season in Egypt.	Hosea 11:1	Matthew 2:14–15
Children would be massacred at Messiah's birthplace.	Jeremiah 31:15	Matthew 2:16–18
A messenger would prepare the way for Messiah.	Isaiah 40:3–5	Luke 3:3–6
Messiah would be rejected by his own people.	Psalm 69:8; Isaiah 53:3	John 1:11; John 7:5
Messiah would be a prophet.	Deuteronomy 18:15	Acts 3:20–22
Messiah would be preceded by Elijah.	Malachi 4:5–6	Matthew 11:13–14
Messiah would be declared the Son of God.	Psalm 2:7	Matthew 3:16–17
Messiah would be called a Nazarene.	Isaiah 11:1	Matthew 2:23
Messiah would bring light to Galilee.	Isaiah 9:1–2	Matthew 4:13–16
Messiah would speak in parables.	Ps.78:2–4; Is. 6:90	Matthew 13:10–15, 34–35
Messiah would be sent to heal the brokenhearted.	Isaiah 61:1–2	Luke 4:18–19
Messiah would be a priest after Melchizedek's order.	Psalm 110:4	Hebrews 5:5–6
Messiah would be called King.	Ps. 2:6; Zech. 9:9	Matt. 27:37; Mark 11:7–11
Messiah would be praised by little children.	Psalm 8:2	Matthew 21:16

Messiah would be betrayed.	Ps. 41:9; Zech. 11:12–13	Luke 22:47; Mt:14–16
Messiah's betrayal money used to buy a potter's field.	Zechariah 11:12–13	Matthew 27:9–10
Messiah would be falsely accused.	Psalm 35:11	Mark 14:57–58
Messiah would be silent before His accusers.	Isaiah 53:7	Mark 15:4–5
Messiah would be spat upon and struck.	Isaiah 50:6	Matthew 26:67
Messiah would be hated without cause.	Psalm 35:19, 69:4	John 15:24–25
Messiah would be crucified with criminals.	Isaiah 53:12	Matthew 27:38; Mark 15:27–28
Messiah would be given vinegar to drink.	Psalm 69:21	Matthew 27:34; John 19:28–30
Messiah's hands and feet would be pierced.	Ps. 22:16; Zech. 12:10	John 20:25–27
Messiah would be mocked and ridiculed.	Psalm 22:7–8	Luke 23:35
Soldiers would gamble for Messiah's garments.	Psalm 22:18	Luke 23:34; Matthew 27:35–36
Messiah's bones would not be broken.	Exodus 12:46; Ps.34:20	John 19:33–36
Messiah would be forsaken by God.	Psalm 22:1	Matthew 27:46
Messiah would pray for his enemies.	Psalm 109:4	Luke 23:34
Soldiers would pierce Messiah's side.	Zechariah 12:10	John 19:34
Messiah would be buried with the rich.	Isaiah 53:9	Matthew 27:57–60
Messiah would resurrect from the dead.	Ps.16:10; Ps. 49:15	Matthew 28:2–7; Acts 2:22–32
Messiah would ascend to heaven.	Psalm 24:7–10	Mark 16:19; Luke 24:51
Messiah would be seated at God's right hand.	Psalm 68:18, 110:1	Mark 16:19; Matthew 22:44
Messiah would be a sacrifice for sin.	Isaiah 53:5–12	Romans 5:6–8

Chapter 2: Recent Creation
Does the Bible Really Say That God Created Everything in Six Days Just 6,000 Years Ago?[19]

See our Video "Young Earth v. Old Earth: What Does the Bible Say?" *www.genesisapologetics.com/helpful-videos/*

In this Chapter, a dialogue between Dan, a seminary student who is currently exploring what he believes about Genesis, and Dave, a seasoned mentor who holds to a "Genesis as history" position presents a Biblical case for recent creation.

DAN: Hi Dave! So my seminary professor said in class today that there are at least four different ways of interpreting the Genesis Creation account. There's the literal/historical "young earth" view, the Day-age view, Progressive Creation, and the Gap Theory.

DAVE: Okay, so which one do you lean toward right now?

DAN: I think there could be some truth in all of them. I mean, does there really have to be only one "correct" view?

DAVE: Well, first of all, think about what you just said. If we say that all views carry truth, that we in effect assert that the view that "all views carry truth" is the correct view. So there's no logical way to avoid asserting some kind of view about a correct view.

DAN: That makes sense. So I guess the better question is which view is correct?

DAVE: I think so. A first step to answering that would involve studying their differences. After all, if each view contains a truth claim that contradicts the other views, then we cannot logically hold contradictory views about the same creation account. In the Historical View, Genesis is taken literally.

DAN: Like saying one day during Creation Week was a real 24-hour day?

DAVE: Exactly. This view also follows the genealogies in Genesis chapters 5 and 10 to accurately date when Adam was born, about 2,000 years before Abraham, or about 6,000 years ago.

DAN: Genealogies?

DAVE: Yes, we'll look at the genealogies next. But first, let's take a look at the *authority* of Scripture. The Bible presents the unchangeable, perfect, and true Words of God Himself, including what God says about the history of our world—history that occurred before the Great Flood of Noah's time thousands of years ago. And, since the Bible says that God cannot lie and that He even honors His Word along with His own name, we ought to treat Scripture with the reverence it deserves.[20] Do we agree on that?

DAN: I think so. At least, I'm willing to think about the Bible in those terms. Now does this mean that God's word has authority over how I live?

DAVE: Yes—that too.

DAN: Well, I definitely think it's possible for the Bible to carry that kind of weight in my life. I'll go with that until I find a reason to change my mind.

DAVE: I think that's a good choice for now. And I think I can show you some reasons why that's a good choice.

DAN: Like what?

DAVE: Like those genealogies. Let's turn to Genesis 5 and see what the Bible says about the patriarchs that lived before Noah's Flood:

Genesis 5: The Family of Adam

And Adam lived **130** years, and begot a son in his own likeness, after his image, and named him Seth. After he begot Seth, the days of Adam were 800 years; and he had sons and daughters. So all the days that Adam lived were 930; and he died. Seth lived **105**, and begot Enosh. After he begot Enosh, Seth lived 807, and had sons and daughters. So all the days of Seth were 912; and he died. Enosh lived **90** years, and begot Cainan. After he begot Cainan, Enosh lived 815 years, and had sons and daughters. So all the days of Enosh were 905 years; and he died. Cainan lived **70** years, and begot Mahalalel. After he begot Mahalalel, Cainan lived 840 years, and had sons and daughters. So all the days of Cainan were 910 years; and he died. Mahalalel lived **65** years, and begot Jared. After he begot Jared, Mahalalel lived 830 years, and had sons and daughters. So all the days of Mahalalel were 895 years; and he died. Jared lived **162** years, and begot Enoch. After he begot Enoch, Jared lived 800 years, and had sons and daughters. So all the days of Jared were 962 years; and he died. Enoch lived **65** years, and begot Methuselah. After he begot Methuselah, Enoch walked with God 300 years, and had sons and daughters. So all the days of Enoch were 365 years. And Enoch walked with God; and he was not, for God took him. Methuselah lived **187** years, and begot Lamech. After he begot Lamech, Methuselah lived 782 years, and had sons and daughters. So all the days of Methuselah were 969 years; and he died. Lamech lived **182** years, and had a son. And he called his name Noah, saying, "This one will comfort us concerning our work and the toil of our hands, because of the ground which the Lord has cursed." After he begot Noah, Lamech lived 595 years, and had sons and daughters. So all the days of Lamech were 777 years; and he died. And Noah was **500** years old, and Noah begot Shem, Ham, and Japheth.

Notice that Genesis 5 lists ten patriarchs that lived before Noah's Flood, and—for each of these patriarchs—their age **before** having the son named, the years they lived **after** having a son, and their **total** years are listed. For example, let's look at Adam, the first one listed:

Age Before Having First Son	Years Lived After Having a Son	Total Years
And Adam lived 130 years, and begot a son in his own likeness, after his image, and named him Seth.	After he begot Seth, the days of Adam were 800 years;	So all the days that Adam lived were 930; and he died.

Taking these ten patriarchs ages at the birth of their named sons gives us an inter-connected, non-overlapping chain that we can use for summing up the years that go straight back to Adam, the very first man created:

Table 4. Genesis 5 Genealogies.

Order	Patriarch	Age at Birth of First Son	Years Lived After Son	Total Age	Sum of Years
1	Adam	130	800	930	130
2	Seth	105	807	912	235
3	Enoch	90	815	905	325
4	Cainan	70	840	910	395
5	Mahalalel	65	830	895	460
6	Jared	162	800	962	622
7	Enoch	65	300	365	687
8	Methuselah	187	782	969	874
9	Lamech	182	595	777	1056
10	Noah	500	450	950	1556

Notice that adding the ages in the "age at birth of first son" column sums to a total of 1,556 years (as shown in the far-right column). Now add Noah's age of 100 when the Flood came. This places the Flood at 1,656 years after Creation. Genesis 10 and 11 provide the next set of genealogies that allow us to move up the timescale to Abraham who lived about 2,000 BC, as shown in the chart below.

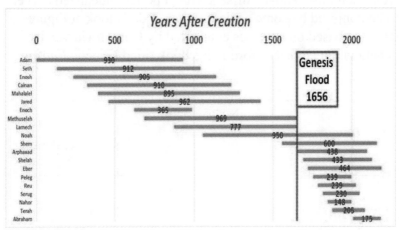

Figure 1. The First 20 Patriarchs since Creation.

Notice that the lifespans of the pre-Flood patriarchs overlapped. Plus, their lifespans declined in a systematic way. These give us confidence that Genesis records an accurate timeline. Summing the time from Adam, the first man created on the Sixth Day of Creation Week, to Abraham is about 2,000 years, then from Abraham to the time of Christ is about another 2,000 years, then we have from Christ until now, another 2,000 years. So, the straight chronology from the Bible places Creation about 6,000 years ago.[21]

DAN: Wait a minute. You're saying that people lived for hundreds of years before the Flood? And some of them over 900 years? How can this support the Bible? This just doesn't seem possible.

DAVE: That's a good question. I think the lifespans in the Bible support the historicity of the Bible much more than challenge its credibility. You see, Moses, who was the man God chose to finalize these texts, was either an expert mathematician who faked biologically significant ages or he wrote down the actual lifespans of the ancient Biblical patriarchs. This is because the declining lifespans of the patriarchs who lived before the Flood and afterwards *fit a naturally declining, downward-curving slope*. It fits a logarithmic decay curve too

35

well, including realistic offsets from a perfect, idealized curve, to be conjured by some ancient writer. Take a look at Figure 2, which is based on analyses conducted by Cornell University geneticist Dr. John Sanford in his book titled *Genetic Entropy*.[22]

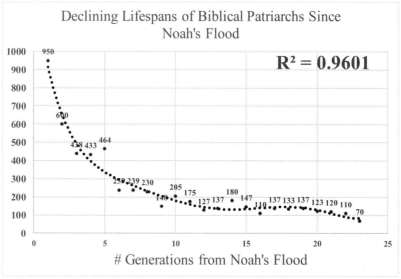

Figure 2. Biologically realistic lifespan decline trend in post-Flood Genesis patriarchs.

As Dr. Sanford points out, the "shape of the downward slope should be immediately recognized by any biologist. It is a biological decay curve."[23] Something happened to the line of Noah's descendants after the Flood—some type of rapid degenerative process that was quite *systematic*.

The Biblical data are internally consistent in a way that chance or an ancient forger would not likely duplicate, since 96% of the data follow a systematic power decay curve.

DAN: So you're saying the shape of the curve is biological—and we can see this better when we plot it on a graph?

DAVE: Exactly. Think about this for a minute—most historians agree that *these data drew from the Bible, and that different authors in different timeframes originally recorded and later transcribed it.* Two plausible explanations describe what we see: Either the data are real and the patriarchs actually lived these recorded ages, or it was carefully invented by some writer thousands of years ago who intentionally mimicked a systematically declining slope.

DAN: Okay, it certainly sounds like the declining lifespans follow a mathematical decline that's not some random occurrence. But what could allow them to live so long before the Flood?

DAVE: Now isn't that the million-dollar question! Nobody knows for sure, since we only have our current lifespans to study. But that doesn't stop folks from offering possibilities. Perhaps external factors such as changes to Earth's atmosphere (e.g., oxygen, pressures, sunlight, etc.) had an effect. Maybe more likely though, internal factors like our declining genetic integrity shrunk human lifespans. I don't think we'll know exactly why we live shorter lives these days until somebody figures out why we age. So far, biologists say that aging is complicated, but that different creatures seem to have set lifespan limits. For example, some small mammals never live longer than a few years, whereas tortoises live several hundred, and some of today's Greenland sharks are over 500 years old.

DAN: That makes sense. But what if there are gaps in those genealogies, allowing for more time to be inserted between them?

DAVE: Scholars have debated the possible gaps for years, but even if there were gaps in these genealogies, we cannot place gaps in their chronologies without basically rewriting the text to fit our own preferences.

DAN: Wait. What's the difference between the genealogy and chronology?

DAVE: So the genealogy considers just their names, but the chronology accounts for the numbers. So even if someone insists that Genesis omitted a few names between two patriarchs, the text still supplies a specific number of years that elapsed between the two given names.

DAN: I see. So gaps or no gaps, we should take the numbers listed as precise records, or else we just start making them "say" whatever we want, and then they lose any meaning.

DAVE: That's exactly right. For example, even many secular historians would agree with Christian scholars that Abraham lived about 2,000 BC, or about 4,000 years ago. So if that's true, with Abraham being the 20th patriarch after Adam listed in the line-up provided in Genesis, we can't have tens of thousands of years' worth of missing genealogies based on the idea that "modern" humans emerged from ape-like ancestors about 50,000 years ago. For example, some creation views agree with the evolutionary timeline that places the evolution of modern humans about 50,000 years ago.[24] With this position, there would be 44,000 years of "missing" genealogies in Genesis! Hardly a reliable record.

DAN: Wow! If the Bible includes the creation of all living things, including humans, which it clearly does, holding to a creation of about 6,000 years ago seems to make sense—at least Biblically.

DAVE: Yes, and the other amazing thing to consider about the lifespans in Genesis is that many of them *overlap*, so there's not a lot of room left for gaps. Further, the Genesis genealogies are repeated in other parts of the Bible, including the books of Ruth, Jude, Matthew, and Luke. This shows that the New Testament and Old Testament's human authors also believed in the Genesis genealogies as real history.

DAN: Okay, so let's say that the genealogies trace back to a literal Adam about 6,000 years ago, but what about the days in the first chapter of Genesis? Couldn't the days themselves be long periods of time? For example, what about when the Bible says "a day to the Lord can be like a thousand years."

DAVE: Ah, yes, 2 Peter 3:8... It actually says that "one day is with the Lord as a thousand years, and a thousand years as one day." But it's talking about God's judgment and His patience with man's rebellion. Notice that the verse says one day is *as* a thousand years. It's a simile showing that God is outside of time, because He is the Creator of time. We know

38

that those who use this verse to say that one creation week day took a thousand years are forcing that view onto the Bible since they never assert the last part of the verse: that a thousand years of Old Testament history all happened in one day.

DAN: So, it's saying that to God time does not affect Him? But to man, a day is still a day?

DAVE: Exactly. It's not defining a day, because it doesn't say, "a day *is* a thousand years." It's not even talking about the days of creation at all. Rather, both times—a day and a thousand years—are described from God's perspective because "with the Lord" these times are the same. The verse is saying that with God, time has no meaning, because He is eternal, outside of the dimension of time that He created. So a thousand years, a day, and a second all are the same to Him. He sees all of history *simultaneously*.

DAN: So, it's a little complicated when people try and define it that way, to try and come up with longer ages.

DAVE: Well, look at it this way: If each day in Genesis 1 was a thousand years, on day three God made the plants, but on day four He made the sun. We know plants need the sun to survive, so if each day was a thousand years, the plants would have all died long before the sun rose on the fourth day.[25] Also, flying insects like bees were created on the fifth day to pollenate plants and trees that were created on the third day. It really makes more sense if all these components of creation were present for it to work as a whole.

DAN: Those are good points. The creation account seems to make more sense if the six days are literal days,

DAVE: Because the word "day" (in Hebrew: *yom*) is used over 2,000 times in the Old Testament, it's important to look at the context in which it's used. In the passage in Peter, the writer is referring back to Psalm 90 verse 4, which says, "For a thousand years in Your sight are like yesterday when it is past, and like a watch in the night," yet a night watch does not last 1,000 years, does it?

DAN: That would be quite a watch! Lots of coffee!

DAVE: Yes, indeed! Here, 1,000 years is just a figure of speech, a comparison to make something more vivid. In context, 2 Peter 3 is saying that although it may seem like a long time to us, the Lord still keeps His promises.

DAN: That's something to be thankful for.

DAVE: So, back to the Hebrew word for "day" (*yom*), yes, it does mean different things in different contexts, but in the first chapter of Genesis, it's rather clear that *yom* is used to mean a literal, 24-hour day. Take a look at Genesis 1:5. It states, "And the **evening** and the **morning** were the **first** day." What stands out to you about that verse?

DAN: Well, I've heard that the Jewish day starts at sundown. So, it sounds like God is starting a new day.

DAVE: Exactly. Here *yom* is used along with evening and morning followed by a number after each of the days of creation, just like the verse you read. And it repeats over and over at the end of each Creation day. This makes them real 24-hour days.

DAN: Okay. But, if God is all-powerful, He could have just created everything in an instant, right? Why six days?

DAVE: I think He was setting up a system of days for us to live in. He was setting up context for our lives and how the world works.

DAN: It all goes back to context—the "why" behind the "what." But what about *yom* being used in other passages as a longer period of time, or an era?

DAVE: First of all, *yom* is used over 400 times in the Old Testament when it's used with a number, like "first day." In every case, it always means an ordinary day.

DAN: So, it's not just in Genesis 1? Wow, that's interesting!

DAVE: It gets better. *Yom* is used with the word "evening" or "morning" 23 times, and "evening" and "morning" appear together without *yom* 38 times, and all 61 times the text refers to an ordinary day. God seemed to want to make it clear to us. He said "evening" and "morning," then a day, and a number. Another thing to consider is that God created time on

Day 1. Before then, time as we know it didn't exist.

DAN: Wow, I never really thought about when God created "time."

DAVE: It's hard to wrap our minds around existence before time. Look here in Genesis 1:14. It says that God established "lights in the firmament of the Heavens to divide the day from the night" and that they would be used for "signs and seasons, and for days and years."

DAN: So, it sounds like God began the measurement of time using days and weeks. Seven days for a week, 24-hours for a day.

DAVE: Exactly. But there's an even bigger issue. All of the non-literal creation stories compromise on the 24-hour day and use long ages instead, even though the Bible is clear God created in an ordinary day timeline.

DAN: That's true. That would mean only one of the views on Genesis could be accurate.

DAVE: Dan, do you believe the Ten Commandments were written by God's own hand?

DAN: I thought Moses chiseled them in stone?

DAVE: Take a look—it says here in Exodus 31:18, "He gave Moses two tablets of the Testimony, tablets of stone, written with the finger of God."

DAN: It looks like God himself wrote the commandments.

DAVE: Yes, and when God wrote about the creation week in the Ten Commandments, He wrote: "For in six days the Lord made the heavens and the earth, the sea, and all that is in them, and rested on the seventh day. Therefore the Lord blessed the Sabbath day and hallowed it" (Exodus 20:11). So there it is again, one book after Genesis…six days. And it's even in the Ten Commandments, *written by the hand of God.*

DAN: Then what do you think God wanted the Israelites to believe when He said this? Long ages or eras? Or real days?

DAVE: Well, God was talking about the Sabbath, which is one day a week. If God meant "thousands of years" when he said "day," then that would make for a really long work week!

DAN: Yes! Too long! So why do really smart Bible scholars try to lengthen creation week's days?

DAVE: I think there are different reasons. It would seem from this passage that God told us what to believe, and what to model our lives after...six days of work, then rest on the seventh. And come to think of it, our weeks have been like this ever since the beginning. After all, we don't have a five-day week, do we? Back in the 1920's the Soviets tried a five-day week and a six-day week, but it was a major failure. So they went back to a seven-day week.

DAN: That's amazing. It seems to be hardwired into human existence. As though God designed us to work six days and take a rest on the seventh.

DAVE: Plus, if you look at the context of the Ten Commandments, it wouldn't make much sense if nine out of the ten commandments are literal, and one is figurative. How could lying, adultery, and stealing be figures of speech. It's pretty black and white—just like the days of Creation.

DAVE: Yes—we certainly don't work for six long ages, but six days, then we rest. God gave us a day of rest to reset our internal clocks. God didn't have to give us that seventh day, but He knew we needed it.

DAN: So what happens when we don't believe in a literal six days?

DAVE: Well, if the days in Genesis 1 are not real days, the only alternative is that Genesis is poetic or figurative.

DAN: Yes, I've heard that from some of my professors.

DAVE: The big challenge is, where does figurative end and truth start? If the genealogies starting with Adam were contrived, and the Earth is much older than 6,000 years, then what? Was Abraham real? The tower of Babel? The Resurrection?

DAN: And whose "truth" is the real truth? I guess it becomes a slippery slope.

DAVE: Unfortunately, it does. Besides, the other views of creation you mentioned emerged in just the last couple of centuries. Before the Enlightenment, the majority of Church

42

teachings held to the historical view of Genesis. Back in 18th century, the elite in society decided they wanted to get away from the Bible and create their own truth. Man became his own God. Unfortunately, it seeped into the Church and continues today. Imagine how these other creation views undermine the authority of Scripture. They insert millions of years that aren't in the text.

DAN: If you allow millions of years, you also allow evolution in?

DAVE: Yes, then "deep time" plus chance and mutations become our creator—rather than God Himself spontaneously creating life out of His sheer power. This compromise on the authority of Scripture certainly doesn't help Christianity. Caving in on Scripture's authority has a huge impact on young people. Think about it, if the Bible isn't true, then there is no moral compass. Truth is relative. And if there's no moral compass, people can make their own reality.

DAN: So, we've been talking about the Old Testament. Is there any support for a literal Creation in the New Testament?

DAVE: Actually, there is. Jesus referred to the Old Testament over 40 times. Every single time He treated the Old Testament literally and historically. For instance, in Mark 10:6 Jesus mentioned that God created man and woman at the "beginning of Creation"—not long ages after Creation. Jesus also references other Old Testament accounts as true events, such as Noah's Flood, the destruction of Sodom and Gomorrah, Jonah and the great fish, and many others.

DAN: And if you really think about it, Jesus was there to witness these events.

DAVE: Exactly. Paul says in Colossians 1 that everything was made by Jesus, through Jesus, and for Jesus. And in Him, all things hold together. Jesus was there to see everything happen.

DAN: Okay, this is all pretty convincing, but why does it matter? What difference does it make if was six days, six thousand years ago, or millions of years ago? All that matters is that we believe in Jesus, right?

DAVE: That's a great question. And there are a lot of great answers. First, those who believe in long ages and those who believe in a young earth both have the same data.

DAN: Then what's the difference? If it's the same data, how do we get such different ideas about the history of life on Earth?

DAVE: Well, one submits to the author of Scripture, relying on Scripture to tell us about the basic framework of the history of the world, our origins, and our purpose. The other assumes it takes billions of years to form the universe, all based on man-made evolutionary views. I choose God-written over man-made, since the God-written framework involved first-hand eyewitnesses and the man-made view reduces to speculations.

DAN: It really does come down to those two choices, doesn't it?

DAVE: Pretty much. Another issue to help discern between them is death before sin.

DAN: Okay. What does that have to do with the gospel?

DAVE: Well, what does the Bible say about the Garden of Eden?

DAN: Perfect world. No death. No suffering.

DAVE: Exactly. It was so great, even God called it "Very Good" after He had created everything. The Bible even says animals and people were vegetarians in the original Creation. Adam and Eve pretty much had free reign on Creation. The only thing God asked them not to do was eat the fruit from the Tree of the Knowledge of Good and Evil. God told them if they ate of that tree, they would surely die.

DAN: Sounds like a great world to live in.

DAVE: No kidding. If death and suffering were around before the Fall, Adam would have had a pretty good idea what God was talking about. He would have seen evidence of death everywhere, and questioned God, "What's the big deal about death if I eat from the forbidden tree—everything's going to die." Because of Adam's sin, death and decay were introduced into the amazing pure world. And still, our sin continues to bring death, suffering, and bloodshed into the world. For example, Romans 5:12 states that sin entered the world through the sin of Adam and Eve. As a result, God cursed our work, the ground with thorns and thistles, and pain in childbearing. Romans 8 says the entire creation is subjected to futility and "groans and labors" under the weight of sin.

DAN: I think I'm getting this. Like entropy. Everything is breaking down. Even across the universe.

DAVE: Yes, and man's sin goes far and wide. But God had a plan to redeem and restore His creation.

DAN: Through Jesus.

DAVE: Exactly. Because of sin and the curse, Jesus had to come and die, breaking the curse of sin for all time. Here's a question: What type of crown did Jesus have on the Cross?

DAN: Wait a minute… it was a crown of thorns. Thorns. The curse. Jesus really was taking the curse of sin on himself at the Cross!

DAVE: So, if Adam and Eve were just fiction and there was no initial sin, the entire reason for Jesus coming down is irrelevant. He died for nothing. There was no curse to redeem us from.

DAN: But that's not what the Bible says. If that's true, then everything we believe is in vain.

DAVE: Exactly! That's why these things are so important. If we believe the Bible from the very first verse, from a perfect world, to the Fall, to redemption, then Jesus' death on the Cross makes perfect sense.

DAN: It really does. It's either death and suffering over millions of years before Adam or a perfect creation marred by original sin only 6,000 years ago.

DAVE: A person can be saved by the Blood of Jesus and still believe in deep time, so we're not talking about a salvation issue. But if they believe in long ages they can't grow fully in their faith because deep time erases the logical foundation for Christ on the cross. My evolution-leaning brothers and sisters, whether they recognize it or not, have to discount a very important part of the Bible and deny some of the teachings of Jesus. By denying the authority of Scripture in their lives, it's going to stunt their spiritual growth.

DAN: Then why do some believers support the long ages idea?

DAVE: My guess is that many of them feel pressured to be accepted by the mainstream, or they just haven't fully thought through why they believe the way they do. Throughout my time as a Christian I've seen many people compromise on the creation account, as well as other parts of Scripture. Most of the time they really don't know how much it's costing them and their families. If we trust the entire Bible as true, then I believe blessings will come to those who completely embrace the whole Scripture. For example, Jesus said, "For whoever is ashamed of Me *and My words*, of him the Son of Man will be ashamed when He comes in His own glory, and in His Father's, and of the holy angels" (Luke 9:26). Many people who compromise on the first page of Scripture are holding back in their faith, sometimes without even being aware they are doing so.

DAN: Wow, that's great insight. Thanks for being patient with me and my questions. I've learned a lot.

DAVE: Wait—before you go—there's just one more thing for you to consider.

DAN: What's that?

DAVE: Well, this one has to do with a reflection more than anything else—it's pretty basic theology. This final thing to consider is what I call the "It makes the most sense" factor when it comes to origins. What I mean is simply this: When you read just the first three chapters of Genesis you see God, an eternal, all-powerful being, creating space, time, matter, and then life—all within a week's time. Then, shortly after these creative events, mankind—whom He had entrusted with free will—gave in to sin, bringing the curse of death into God's perfect creation, and along with it, bloodshed, disease, and suffering. Then, less than 1,700 years after Creation, God hit the "reset" button by causing the Flood, totally wiping out the first version of the world He had created. So, if these events really happened in history, don't you think that God's solution to the fallen state of the world would have included some hints that the Savior (His Son) would reverse these same *specific* negative effects that sin brought into the world?

DAN: Wait, I thought you said this was going to be easy...

DAVE: It is, actually—just stay with me. Look at it this way: If God was going to send a Savior into a world that was cursed in *specific* ways from the Fall, don't you think it would make sense that the Savior would reverse those very *specific* effects? For example:

- Sin brought **death**; Jesus raised the dead, and raised Himself from the grave.
- Sin brought **corruption** of God's original perfect design; Jesus healed the sick and cured diseases.
- The curse of sin brought **thorns and thistles** to plant life; Jesus triumphed over the curse of sin while wearing a crown of thorns on the Cross.
- Sin brought the first **bloodshed** (with God killing an animal to make a covering for Adam and Eve); Jesus was the last blood sacrifice necessary for our sins.
- All of **Creation groans** under the weight of sin (Romans 8); Jesus will redeem all of creation unto Himself (Colossians 1).

There's even something else—one of the first creative works by God recorded in Genesis 1:3 is the spreading of light onto the formless mass of the Earth: "Then God said, 'Let there be **light**'; and there was **light**." Now, isn't it interesting that John 1:1–8 says the following about Jesus?

In the **beginning** was the Word, and the Word was with God, and the Word was God. He was in the **beginning** with God. **All things were made through Him, and without Him nothing was made that was made**. In Him was life, and the life was the **light** of men. And the **light** shines in the darkness, and the darkness did not comprehend it. There was a man sent from God, whose name was John. This man came for a witness, to bear witness of the **Light**, that all through him might believe. He was not that Light, but was sent to bear witness of that **Light**. That was the **true Light** which gives **light** to every man coming into the world.

Do you see now how Jesus's redemptive acts specifically fit into Genesis, like a hand-in-glove? It's like God knew exactly how to redeem the Earth and His people by removing the *specific* effects of the Fall…

DAN: Looking at it this way, it seems like God has a very cohesive plan for redemption spelled out through Scripture!

Chapter 3: Dating Rocks
Does Radiometric Dating Really Prove That the Earth Is Billions of Years Old?

Secular scientists date the Earth to about 4.5 billion years old by using selected radiometric dating results. Ultimately, this "deep time" serves as the very *foundation* of evolution theory. High school biology books openly acknowledge this necessary connection:

> Evolution takes a long time. If life has evolved, then Earth must be very old. Geologists now use radioactivity to establish the age of certain rocks and fossils. This kind of data could have shown that the Earth is young. If that had happened, Darwin's ideas would have been refuted and abandoned. Instead, radioactive dating indicates that Earth is about 4.5 billion years old—plenty of time for evolution and natural selection to take place.[26]

As discussed in previous chapters, this secular viewpoint contradicts God's stated word in Genesis and even the Ten Commandments, where He wrote with His own hand that He created the heavens, Earth, sea, and all that is in them in six days (Exodus 20:11).

The entire belief regarding the age of the earth rests upon evolution's required time, bolstered by radiometric dating. That's sure putting a lot of faith in something that can't be tested through direct observation. After all, plenty of assumptions go into the calculations, as we'll discuss in this chapter.

Keep in mind that while this chapter reviews the technical details behind radiometric dating, only two very basic, but completely catastrophic "fatal flaws" undermine radiometric dating.

The **first fatal flaw** is that it relies upon *untestable assumptions*. The entire practice of radiometric dating stands or falls on the veracity of four *untestable* assumptions. The assumptions are untestable because we cannot go back millions of years to verify the findings done today in a laboratory, and we cannot go back in time to test the original conditions in which the rocks were formed. If these assumptions that underlie radiometric dating are not true, then the entire theory falls flat, like a chair without its four legs.

The **second fatal flaw** clearly reveals that at least one of those assumptions must actually be wrong because radiometric dating *fails to correctly date rocks of known ages*. For example, in the case of Mount St. Helens, we can watch the rocks being formed in the 1980s, but when sent to a laboratory for dating, they return ages of "hundreds of thousands" to "millions of years" old for a 10-year-old rock. Similarly, some rocks return radiometric "ages" twice as old as the accepted age for earth. Most rocks return conflicting radiometric "ages." In all these cases, researchers tend to select results that match what they already believe about earth's age (see Table 5 for details of this study, and several others like it).

Overview of Radiometric Dating[27]

Fossil remains are found in sedimentary rock layers. Layers of sediment are formed when various size particles (e.g., dirt, rocks, and vegetation) accumulate in places such as deserts, rivers, lakes, and the ocean. Most texts teach that it takes a long time for these sediments to build up, with older layers buried beneath younger layers. Fossils found in lower layers are deemed to be older than those in the upper layers, older on the bottom younger on the top. This is called relative age dating. To help establish the relative ages of rock layers that are not directly related to one another and their fossils, evolutionary scientists use *index fossils*.

Index fossils are distinct fossils, usually of an extinct organism, used to establish and correlate the relative ages of rock layers. Index fossils typically have a short stratigraphic or vertical range. This means they are found in only one or a few layers, though that layer or layers outcrops in many places—at least that's the theory. In reality, many index fossils occur above or below their expected ranges. Evolutionists assume that the creature evolved somehow, lived for a certain time period, and then died out. Textbooks are correct when they state that relative dating provides no information whatsoever about a fossil's absolute age. Nevertheless, most textbook writers and the scientists they cite all grew up with a belief in uniformitarian geologic processes. The principle of uniformity is a philosophy and an assumption that the slow geologic processes going on today must explain the deposits of the past. They teach the motto, "the present is the key to the past." It's not. Eyewitness records are a better key to the past. Also, keen observations in the field testify that the sediments comprising the ancient rock layers were laid down *catastrophically*, not slowly over millions of years.

Today, the geologic time scale shows ages based on radiometric age dating. Many textbook authors consider radiometric ages as absolute ages. However, as you will soon learn, these techniques stray far from absolute dates, though they may reveal relative ages of some rocks.

The Age of the Earth

Today's evolutionists base their age of the Earth on an interpretation of radioactive elements. They give the age of 4.5 billion years and the various rock layers are given names with assigned ages (Figure 3). Those who believe these ever-changing but always unimaginably old age assignments call each rock system a "period." The names help, but these ages are far from absolute. To understand exactly why, we must first learn the basics of radioactive elements, and of the techniques used when treating these systems of elements as clocks.

Many elements on the periodic table have radioactive forms. Stable atoms have a set number of protons, neutrons, and

51

orbital electrons. Isotopes are atoms of the same elements with the same number of protons but different numbers of neutrons. Some isotopes are radioactive and others are stable. A radioactive nucleus is not stable and will change, or transmutate, into another element over time by emitting particles and/or radiation.

EON	ERA	PERIOD	EPOCH	Alleged Age Years	Young Earth Evidences
Phanerozoic — This is where most fossils occur	Cenozoic	Quaternary	Holocene	10,000	
			Pleistocene	2,600,000	Soft Frog with bloody bone marrow
		Tertiary	Pliocene	5,300,000	Salamander muscle
			Miocene	23,000,000	
			Oligocene	30,900,000	⇐ Young coal, Penguin feathers, Lizard skin
			Eocene	55,800,000	
			Paleocene	65,500,000	
	Mesozoic	Cretaceous		145,500,000	⇐ Young Diamonds Young Coal
		Jurassic		201,600,000	Dinosaur DNA, blood, blood vessels and protein
		Triassic		251,000,000	
	Paleozoic	Permian		299,000,000	
		Pennsylvanian		318,000,000	⇐ Young Coal
		Mississippian		359,000,000	
		Devonian		416,000,000	
		Silurian		444,000,000	
		Ordovician		488,000,000	
		Cambrian		542,000,000	
Precambrian	Proterozoic Eon				⇐ Helium in zircon crystals
				2,500,000,000	
	Archean Eon			3,850,000,000	

Figure 3. Uniformitarian Geologic Time Scale (with problems noted). The time scale is placed vertically because older sedimentary deposits are buried beneath younger sedimentary deposits. The assumption of slow geologic processes and radiometric age dating has drastically inflated the age of the Earth and its strata.

A basic way to express the rate of radioactive decay is called the half-life. This equals the length of time needed for 50% of a quantity of radioactive material to decay. Unstable radioactive isotopes called parent elements decay into (or give birth to) stable elements called daughter elements. Each radioactive element has its own specific half-life (see Table 5).

Table 5: Radiometric Isotopes and Half-Lives.

Examples of Radioactive Isotopes that Change into Stable Elements		
Radioactive Parent Element	Stable Daughter Element	Half-Life
Carbon-14 (^{14}C)	Nitrogen-14 (^{14}N)	5,730 Years
Potassium-40 (^{40}K)	Argon-40 (^{40}Ar)	1.3 Billion Years
Uranium-238 (^{238}U)	Lead-206 (^{206}Pb)	4.5 Billion Years
Rubidium-87 (^{87}Rb)	Strontium-87 (^{87}Sr)	48.6 Billion Years

Note: Carbon-14 is not used to date minerals or rocks, but is used for organic remains that contain carbon, such as wood, bone, or shells.

To estimate a radioisotope age of a crystalline rock, geologists measure the ratio between radioactive parent and stable daughter products in the rock or, in particular, minerals of the rock. They then use a model to convert the measured ratio into an age estimate. The models incorporate key assumptions, like the ratio of parent to daughter isotopes in the originally formed rock. Could those models' assumptions contain errors?

Igneous rocks—those that have formed from molten magma or lava—are the primary rock types analyzed to determine radiometric ages. For example, let's assume that when an igneous rock solidified, a certain mineral in it contained 1,000 atoms of radioactive potassium (^{40}K) and zero atoms of argon (^{40}Ar). After one half-life of 1.3 billion years, the rock would contain 500 ^{40}K and 500 ^{40}Ar atoms, since 50% has decayed. This is a 500:500 or 500-parent:500-daughter ratio, which reduces to a 1:1 ratio. If the sample contained this ratio, then the rock would be declared to be 1.3 billion years old. If the ratio is greater than 1:1, then not even one half-life has expired, so the rock would be younger. However, if the ratio is less than 1:11, then the rock is considered older than the half-life for that system.

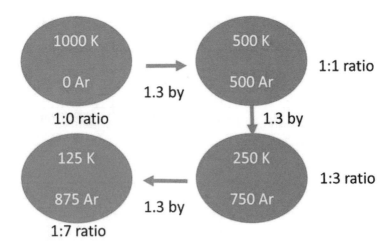

Figure 4. Decay of Radioactive potassium-40 to argon-40. "By" means "billions of years," K is potassium, Ar is argon. After three half-lives of this system, totaling 3.9 billion years, only 125 of the original set of 1000 radioactive potassium-40 atoms remain, assuming even decay for all that time.

Age-dating a rock requires at least these four basic assumptions:

1. Laboratory measurements that have no human error or misjudgments;
2. The rock began with zero daughter element isotopes;

3. The rock maintained a "closed system;" (defined below) and

4. The decay rate remained constant.

Let's describe each of these.

1. Measuring the radioactive parent and stable daughter elements to obtain the ratio between them must be accurate, and it usually is. Keep in mind that most laboratory technicians have been trained in a belief of an old Earth, which may set preconceived ideas about the time periods they expect. They all memorized the typical geologic time scale before they approached their research, and thus may not have an open mind to the idea that the accurately measured isotope ratios may have come from processes other than radioisotope decay.

2. Next, this technician assumes that all the radioactive parent isotopes began decaying right when the mineral crystallized from a melt. He also assumes none of the stable daughter element was present at this time. How can anyone really know the mineral began with 100% radioactive parent and 0% daughter elements? What if some stable daughter element was already present when the rock formed? In fact, geologic literature reveals countless instances when experts explain away unexpected radioisotope age results using the excuse that daughter or parent isotopes must have been present when the rock formed. If so, then those isotopes can indicate nothing of a rock's age.

3. A closed system means that no extra parent or daughter elements have been added or removed throughout the history of the rock. Have you ever seen an atom? Of course not. It is too small, but we must think about this assumption on an atomic level. For example, decay byproducts like argon and helium are both gases. Neither gas tends to attach to any other atom, meaning

55

they rarely react with other chemicals. Instead of reacting with atoms in rock crystals, they build up in rock systems and can move in and out of the rocks. One leading expert in isotope geology states that most minerals do not even form in closed systems. He emphasizes that for a radioactive-determined date to be true, the mineral must be in a closed system.[28] Is there any such thing as a closed system when speaking of rocks?

4. The constant-decay rate assumption involves the decay rate remaining the same throughout the history of the rock. Lab experiments have shown that most changes in temperature, pressure, and the chemical environment have very little effect on decay rates. These experiments have led researchers to have great confidence that this is a reasonable assumption, but it may not hold true. Is the following quote an overstatement of known science? "Radioactive transmutations must have gone on at the present rates under all the conditions that have existed on Earth in the geologic past."[29] Some scientists have found incredible evidence in zircon minerals showing that excessive levels of radioactive decay occurred in the past, as discussed below.

Consider a burning candle sitting on the table. How long has that candle been burning? We can calculate the answer if we know the candle's *burn rate history* and *original length*. However, if the original length is not known, or if it cannot be verified that the burning rate has been constant, it is impossible to tell for sure how long the candle was burning. A similar problem occurs with radiometric dating of rocks. Since the initial physical state of the rock is unknowable, the age can only be estimated according to certain assumptions."[30]

Brand New Rocks Give Old "Ages"

There is now a great abundance of evidence in the scientific literature about rocks giving ages much older than they really are. Warnings go back to the late 1960s and 1970s, but most of the scientific community is still not paying attention. Radiogenic argon and helium contents of recent basalt lava erupted on the deep ocean floor from the Kilauea volcano in Hawaii were measured. Researchers calculated up to 22,000,000 years for brand new rocks![31] The problem is common (see Table 6).

Table 6: Young Volcanic Rocks with Really Old Whole-Rock K-Ar Model Ages.[32]

Lava Flow, Rock Type, and Location	Year Formed or Known Age	^{40}K-^{40}Ar "Age"
Kilauea Iki basalt, Hawaii	AD 1959	8,500,000 years
Volcanic bomb, Mt. Stromboli, Italy	AD 1963	2,400,000 years
Mt. Etna basalt, Sicily	AD 1964	700,000 years
Medicine Lake Highlands obsidian, Glass Mountains, California	<500 years	12,600,000 years
Hualalai basalt, Hawaii	AD 1800–1801	22,800,000 years
Mt. St. Helens dacite lava dome, Washington	AD 1986	350,000 years

The oldest real age of these recent volcanic rocks is less than 500 years. But people witnessed the molten lava solidify into most of these rocks just decades ago. In fact, many of these were only about 10 years old or less when tested. And yet ^{40}K-^{40}Ar dating gives ages from 350,000 to >22,800,000 years.

Potassium-Argon (^{40}K-^{40}Ar) has been the most widespread method of radioactive age-dating for the Phanerozoic rocks, where most of the fossils occur. The misdated rocks shown above violate the initial condition assumption of no radiogenic argon (^{40}Ar) present when the igneous rock formed. However, just like the helium problem, there is too much ^{40}Ar present in recent lava flows, so the method gives excessively old ages for recently formed rocks. The amounts of argon in these rocks indicate they carry isotope "ages" much, much older than their known ages. Could the argon they measured have come from a source other than radioactive potassium decay? If so, then geologists have been trusting a faulty method. If they can't obtain correct values for rocks of known ages, then why should we trust the values they obtain for rocks of unknown ages?

These wrong radioisotope ages violate the initial condition assumption of zero (0%) radioactive argon present when the rock formed. Furthermore, there was insufficient time since cooling for measurable amounts of ^{40}Ar to have accumulated in the rock, due to the slow radioactive decay of ^{40}K. Therefore, radiogenic argon (^{40}Ar) was *already present* in the rocks as they formed.

Radiometric age dating should no longer be sold to the public as providing reliable, absolute ages. Excess argon invalidates the initial condition assumption for potassium dating, and excess helium invalidates the closed-system assumption for uranium dating. The ages shown on the uniformitarian geologic time scale should be removed.

"Young" Fossils in "Old" Mud

The Ono Formation near Redding in northern California has been scoured by researchers and described in scientific publications for more than 140 years. Because the area has millions of fossils (including the much sought after ammonites) and fossilized wood trapped in the same mudflow layers (which Creationists believe are from the Flood), it provides a unique opportunity for carbon dating because they were trapped by the same catastrophic event.

Dr. Andrew Snelling (Geologist) gathered four samples of ammonites and wood buried and fossilized together in the solidified mudstone in this area and sent them to the IsoTrace Radiocarbon Laboratory at the University of Toronto, Canada for dating analysis.[33] The results are summarized in Table 7.

Table 7. Ono Formation Radiocarbon Dating Results.

Dating Results from Ammonites and Wood Fossils in the Ono Formation (Snelling, 2008)			
Specimen	Rock layers	Ammonites	Wood
Dating	112 to 120 Million (conventional age)	36,400 to 48,710 carbon years	32,780 to 42,390 carbon years

Because the ammonites and wood fossils came from a rock unit conventionally regarded as 112 to 120 million years old, the fossils are also claimed to be that old. Such an age far exceeds the limit of the radioactive carbon (^{14}C) method (which is less than 100,000 years). In other words, if these fossils are really over 100 million years old, then there should have been absolutely no measurable ^{14}C in them—but there was—enough to produce easily measurable ages of 32,000 to 48,000 years!

Scientists who believe in long ages assert that the ammonites and wood samples were contaminated with modern carbon in the ground, during sampling, or even in the laboratory. But this study took extensive steps to guard against such contamination. So how can 36,000 carbon-year-old ammonites and 32,000 carbon-year-old wood be stuck in a mudflow of 112 million or more conventional years? Either:

1. One of the three dates is correct and the other two are wrong.
2. All three of the dates are wrong.

If Biblical history is accurate, and we believe that it is, then the second option is the correct choice—*none of the dates are correct.* The fact that measurable ^{14}C existed in the ammonites and wood fossils shows that they are very young– certainly not 112–120 million years old. But how can they still outdate the Biblical age of Creation of about 6,000 years? A number of factors help explain this, including the Earth's stronger magnetic field in the recent past (which changes the atmospheric ^{14}C production rate), and "because the recent Genesis Flood removed so much carbon from the biosphere and buried it, the measured apparent radiocarbon ages are still much higher than the true ages of the fossil ammonites and wood."[34]

Therefore, the true ages of the ammonites and wood are consistent with their burial during the Genesis Flood (about 4,400 years ago), when muddy waters washed sediments and ammonites onto this continental land.

Figure 5. Fossil Ammonites in Rock Concretions in the Ono Formation, California.

Next, we'll take a closer look at the reliability of carbon dating.

Is Carbon Dating Reliable?

Carbon dating assigns ages to organic materials such as wood, bone, teeth, and shells. Evolutionary researchers do not use it to age-date inorganic rocks. Recall that the way scientists use radioisotope dating is by first measuring the ratio of radioactive parent versus stable versions of an element. Carbon dating works by basing an age calculation on the ratio of radioactive carbon (^{14}C) to normal carbon (^{12}C) in the atmosphere before nuclear bomb testing. Carbon-14 decays to nitrogen, not carbon. Using a formula that compares that ratio to a standard modern ratio produces a "percent modern carbon" pMC value that scientists use to estimate carbon ages for carbon-containing materials.

Carbon-14 doesn't decay linearly, but instead decays fast at first, then more slowly later, according to a predictable pattern that can be expressed in units called half-life. Given the short ^{14}C half-life of 5,730 years (see Table 5: Radiometric Isotopes and Half Lives), organic materials purportedly older than 100,000 years (nearly 18 half-lives) should contain absolutely no detectable ^{14}C. However, coal, diamonds, and even dinosaur bones contain plenty of ^{14}C.[35] Carbon dating of historical objects of known age is only (somewhat) accurate back to about 1,000 BC.[36]

The process of Carbon-14 dating includes sound science—observation and repeatable methods. Further, the process uses high-tech laboratory equipment that costs millions. So the method itself is not the issue—it's the *assumptions* that are made when the raw isotope ratio gets converted to calendar years that carbon dating becomes unreliable and inaccurate, especially in its oldest settings. While carbon dating can in fact return somewhat accurate ages for items that are a couple thousand years old (see discussion and endnotes below), too many assumptions accompany carbon dates for items into the deeper past. Several unknown factors can seriously impact carbon ratios. Just a partial list of these factors includes:

1. **Forest fires**. Massive forest fires can change $^{14}C/^{12}C$ ratios much in the same way that volcanic eruptions have.[37] Do we have a complete record of forest fires dating back thousands of years?

2. **Atomic activity/releases**. Atomic bomb testing *doubled* the amount of Carbon-14 in the 1950s and 1960s. Professor Nalini Nadkarni, an ecologist at The Evergreen State College in Washington stated that this testing caused: "a tremendous spike of Carbon-14 — actually 100 percent more Carbon-14 coming into the atmosphere than what we'd had previous to those atom bomb tests."[38] Researchers have found clever ways to normalize measurements to pre-bomb levels, but these extra complications may add more uncertainty to radiocarbon-based age assignments.

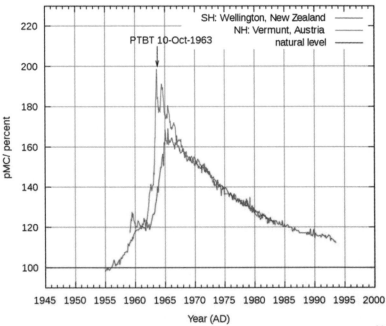

Figure 6. Effect of Atomic Bomb Testing on Carbon Dating.[39]

3. **Volcanic eruptions.** When volcanoes erupt, they eject enormous amounts of carbon into the air. Because

geological carbon does not have detectable ^{14}C, the $^{14}C/^{12}C$ ratio in the area becomes seriously disrupted—in some cases even making *living* plants appear to be 1,000 years old![40] How would a recent past of high volcanism, as shown by ancient lava fields, ash falls, and dead volcanoes, have affected ancient carbon isotope ratios?

4. **Industrialization**. It is widely accepted that the mass burning of coal during the industrial revolution released an enormous amount of ^{12}C into the air, which changed the $^{14}C/^{12}C$ ratio in the atmosphere. Tree-ring studies can give some level of insight into the $^{14}C/^{12}C$ ratio before the industrial revolution, and modern carbon dating takes this into account by running experimental measurements through a calibration formula.[41] But how do we know what the ratio was like thousands of years ago? We simply don't. The entire validity of the dating system hangs on these types of assumptions![42]

5. **Solar flares**. Several studies have shown: 1) significant solar flares have occurred in the past, and 2) these flares have an impact on carbon levels in the atmosphere. For example, in AD 774–775 there was an increase of 1.2% in the ^{14}C content of tree rings, which was about 20 times as high as the background rate of variation.[43] This "spike" was followed by a decline that lasted several years. The cause of this difference is thought to be a solar flare, as the same signal is found in ^{14}C in tree rings around the world, including Germany, Russia, the United States, and New Zealand.[44] Other researchers have noted similar findings.[45] Do we know whether other solar flares like this occurred thousands of years ago?

6. **The Reservoir Effect**. Heavy or light carbon atoms can become trapped, or at least concentrated, in "carbon reservoirs" where carbon isotopes do not quickly equilibrate with the atmosphere's steady level.[46] As a result, some modern deep ocean organics show a carbon

age of 1,500 carbon years, for example. Nearby limestone can also affect carbon isotope concentrations, giving false ages—or at least ages that need even more corrections.

7. **Partial pressure**. Geologic indicators show that atmospheric CO_2 levels were much higher in the past.[47] How might this have affected the carbon isotope ratios?

8. **Magnetic field**. Extrapolated geomagnetic field decay measurements show that just several thousand years ago, Earth's magnetic field may have been twice as strong as today.[48] This may well have altered the rate at which cosmic radiation collides with gas particles in the upper atmosphere—the basis for ^{14}C formation.

When scientists attempt to stretch the results of carbon dating back many thousands of years, are any of these assumptions above being violated? How can we know without being there? Without written records that described these phenomena? A final factor to consider when it comes to carbon dating is the worldwide Flood described in Genesis 6–9, plus the recent Ice Age that followed right after the Flood. Noah's Flood would have uprooted and buried entire forest systems, decreasing the release of ^{12}C into the atmosphere through the decay of vegetation. Creation scientists have looked into this, and believe the Flood explains why most dinosaur bones typically cluster between 17,850 to 49,470 radiocarbon years.[49]

Finally, a key study conducted in 1989 by the British Science and Engineering Research Council (BSERC) arose over concern about the practice of carbon dating. Many results continued to come back with varying dates for various artifacts of known ages (i.e., artifacts which could be reliably dated using written history). So BSERC decided to conduct an *international blind test* on the practice of carbon dating itself. The test was conducted by sending dated artifacts of "known age" to 38 of the world's leading radiocarbon testing laboratories. The results of the study were amazing:[50]

The British Science and Engineering Research Council (which funded the installation of the C14 apparatus at Oxford) ran a series of tests in 1989 with 38 laboratories involved worldwide. As a consequence, the council has insisted this year (1990) on new quality-control measures, by which checks are made with standard reference materials of known age. Of the mass spectrometry technique used at Oxford, Dr. Baxter reports: 'It came out very badly in the survey, even when dating samples as little as 200 years old.' Only 7 out of 38 laboratories produced satisfactory results, and the margin of error with artefacts of known age was two or three times greater than the technique's practitioners claim. *Nature* (the magazine which published details of the original C14 experiment) has now published a demonstration that the radiocarbon technique is not only unsound but also outdated. The Geological Observatory of Columbia University in New York has proved that the C14 results given in past years are in error by as much as 3,500 years in dating fossils, artefacts and events of the past 40,000 years, and the further back we go in time, the greater the error. Dr. Fairbanks of the observatory staff points out that since the C14 dating depends on the ever-variable quantity of C14 in the atmosphere produced by cosmic rays, any alteration of that production either by nature, or by the solar system, or by man-made interference (such as thermo-nuclear bombs) must cause a collapse of the whole hypothesis. He quotes the significant underestimation of the age of ancient objects and states that in a large number of tests C14 failed consistently, the samples being far older than the C14 findings showed.

How can carbon dating be regarded as scientifically reliable and accurate when 0 of 38 laboratories "achieved a correct date, even with plus or minus tolerances, and many were off by *thousands of years*"? Do we know about all the forest fires and volcanic eruptions that have occurred in the distant past? Atomic activity? Solar flares and cycles? Earth's magnetic field? There are so many assumptions required to journey into the distant past—it's a better idea to trust the Creator for our past, and not secular science.

Chapter 4: Dinosaurs
How Do Dinosaurs Fit into the Bible?

See our Dinosaur Video: *www.genesisapologetics.com/dinosaurs/*

The secular viewpoint on dinosaurs directly opposes what the Bible teaches. In a nutshell, the secular idea is that dinosaurs evolved through death of the unfit and survival of the fittest random mutants starting about 220 million years ago and ending at a supposed extinction event about 65 million years ago. This view invokes the trinity of time, chance, and death as the *creators* of dinosaurs.

But according to biblical history, dinosaurs were intentionally designed by God, each made to reproduce after its own kind, and were spontaneously placed on Earth just thousands of years ago. The following Bible passages outline some dinosaur basics:

1. God created **all living things**. Therefore, God created dinosaurs (Genesis 1; Exodus 20:11; Colossians 1:16; John 1:3).
2. God created all land-dwelling, air-breathing animals on the **6th Day** of Creation, right before He created man (Genesis 1:24–25).
3. Tallying the genealogies in Genesis 1–11, this 6th Day occurred about **6,000 years ago**, so dinosaurs were placed here fully-formed (in several different "kinds") at that time.
4. Adam's first job from God was to name **all** the animals (including dinosaurs) after they were **all** created (Genesis 2:20).
5. After God created all animals, He gave Adam and Eve the charge of **taking dominion over every living creature**: "Be fruitful and multiply; fill the earth and subdue it; have dominion over the fish of the sea, over

the birds of the air, and over **every living thing** that moves on the earth" (v. 28). All of God's creatures were present when this dominion order was given.

6. The book of Job describes two dinosaur-like creatures: **Leviathan** and **Behemoth**. Behemoth is given the title of God's "chief" or "first in rank" over all God's creative works (Job 40:19). A plain interpretation of the 13 characteristics that describe this animal match a sauropod dinosaur that was "made along with" man (verse 40:15).

7. All land-dwelling, air-breathing animals **died in a worldwide Flood** (except those on Noah's Ark) about 4,400 years ago (Genesis 6:7, 7:20–23). Part of the reason for this worldwide extinction event was that "all flesh" (including animals) had "corrupted their way on the Earth" (Genesis 6:12).

8. Not all animal "kinds" that got off the Ark after the Flood survived for long in the new, post-Flood world (e.g., many dinosaurs). While we don't know the details, many animal kinds (and probably most of the dinosaurs) **quickly went extinct** after the Flood. Some dinosaurs, however, survived for centuries after the Flood, and contributed to the dragon myths and legends that exist all over the world.[51]

Which of these two viewpoints on dinosaurs is correct? Were all varieties of dinosaurs the products of time, chance, and "survival of the fittest" millions of years ago? Or, were they placed here by an intentional, all-powerful God who spoke them into existence, and then later wiped out in the Global Flood described in Genesis? In this chapter, we'll explore evidence that shows that the latter idea just might be true…

12 Evidences that Align Dinosaurs with the Bible

There are 12 reasons that dinosaurs can provide evidence that the historical view of Genesis (summarized above) is accurate. Rather than dinosaurs being used to "prove" evolution, data surrounding the dinosaur fossil record actually fits the "biblical hypothesis" better than the one provided by evolution! The 12 reasons we'll cover in this section include:

Dinosaurs:

1. Are cleverly designed.
2. Are lacking in both *ancestors* and *transitions* in the fossil record, showing they were spontaneously placed here by God.
3. Were better designed for the first "version" of the Earth (the pre-Flood world).
4. Are part of a vast fossil record, indicating a massive catastrophe like Noah's Flood.
5. Were buried *furiously* (disarticulated).
6. Were *quickly* buried in mud.
7. Were buried *simultaneously*—fleeing in groups.
8. Are frequently found mixed together with marine fossils.
9. Are frequently found buried without juveniles.
10. Have at least 14 "fresh" biomaterials in their bones that cannot last for millions of years.
11. Have carbon-14 in their bones.
12. Have been found in pristine "mummified" condition.

Let's take a brief look at each of these evidences.

Evidence #1: Clever Design

Some dinosaur design features are just plain astounding. We'll explore these fantastic creatures by focusing on two: Triceratops and Sauropods.

Triceratops

Figure 7. Triceratops[52]

Let's make a reasonable assumption that the two massive horns (up to four feet long) protruding from its skull had a purpose—such as ramming either for defensive purposes or against other triceratops for mating rights.[53] How is it possible to mount a head that weighed a couple thousand pounds that was over eight feet long[54] onto a body that could run over 30 miles-per-hour,[55] and still allow it to turn around every which way? The occipital condyle—that's how! Take a look at the perfectly round ball that's on the bottom of the Triceratops skull in Figure 8.

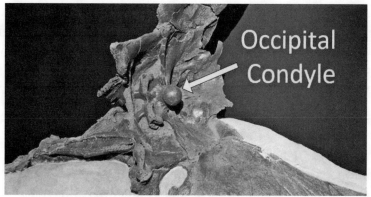

Figure 8. Occipital Condyle[56]

    The occipital condyle is a hard, round-shaped bone that protrudes from the base of the skull that mounts to the anterior end of the spine—just like a trailer ball-and-hitch design.

Figure 9. Trailer Hitch[57]

    The head of a Triceratops was among the largest of all land animals, with some making up one-third of the entire length of the dinosaur's body. In fact, the largest Triceratops skull ever found has an estimated length of 8.2 feet,[58] indicating it could have weighed thousands of pounds by some estimates. The occipital condyle enables the massive head of the Triceratops to be mounted securely to its body in a way that allows it to rotate while this massive beast rammed its head into other dinosaurs! That takes some engineering!

Where are all the semi-Triceratops fossils with "evolving" occipital condyles? They simply don't exist. When these creatures are found in the fossil record, they all have nicely-shaped occipital condyles. It's seems like it was a very good design plan right from the start.

Sauropods

Next, let's take a look at the sauropod dinosaurs. Sauropods are the largest land animals in history, with some of them (such as *Argentinosaurus* and *Patagotitan mayorum*) exceeding 115 feet and weighing over 140,000 pounds.[59]

Figure 10. Sauropod Dinosaur[60]

Figure 11 shows a leg from a massive sauropod dinosaur. Do you notice how the bone at the top (the humerus) is made of one solid piece, followed by the two bones below the knee (the ulna and radius), followed by five foot bones, then five toes? This "large and solid" to "smaller and spread out" system allowed these massive creatures to distribute their weight and walk on mobile pillars. Given that estimates of some sauropods exceed 120 feet and 140,000 pounds, it would certainly take an amazing design plan for this creature to walk! Unlike other dinosaurs, sauropods could lock their legs, conserving energy.

Figure 11. Royal Terrell Museum (Author)

Where are all of the sauropods that don't have this weight-bearing design? They don't exist. All ~300 that have been found so far are made this way.[61] As we'll soon see, this is just the tip of the iceberg when it comes to the design features that need to be present *at the same time* for these creatures to live.

Job 40 and the Behemoth

It's no wonder that the Book of Job (the oldest book of the Bible, written about 3,500 years ago[62]) refers to Behemoth—a sauropod dinosaur—as the "chief" or "first in rank" of all God's creation. Consider the description of this animal from Job 40:6–24:

> Then the Lord answered Job out of the whirlwind, and said: "Now prepare yourself like a man; I will question you, and you shall answer Me... Look at Behemoth, which I **made along with you** and which feeds on grass like an ox. What **strength it has in its loins**, what **power in the muscles of its belly!** Its **tail sways like a cedar**; the **sinews of its thighs are close-knit.** Its **bones are tubes of bronze**, its **limbs like rods of iron**. It **ranks first among the works of God,** yet its Maker can approach it with his sword. The hills bring it their produce, and all the wild animals play nearby. Under the lotus plants it lies, hidden among the reeds in the marsh. The lotuses conceal it in their shadow; the poplars by the stream surround it. **A raging river does not alarm it; it is secure, though the Jordan should surge against its mouth.** Can anyone capture it by the eyes, or trap it and pierce its nose?

In context, Job and his philosopher friends just finished over 30 chapters of dialogue trying to explain God and why He would allow such hardships into Job's life. Then God shows up in a whirlwind, tells Job to "brace himself like a man" and says that He would be the one asking Job the questions for a while (KJV: "Gird up thy loins now like a man: I will demand of thee, and declare thou unto me"). Then, for four chapters straight, God asks Job 77 rhetorical questions that are all about Creation. After explaining to Job that He is the master designer of space and earth, God describes 13 of His created animals, such as an ostrich, horse, and deer, then caps off the discussion by telling Job about His two grandest creations: Behemoth and Leviathan. God calls Behemoth the "first of all of His ways," using the Hebrew term (re'shiyth), which means *first in a rank*, the *chief*, the *most supreme* of His creative works.

When God says to Job, sit down, brace yourself, and now I will tell you of the chief of all my works—the biggest, most amazing land creature I ever made—he's not talking about a common animal like a hippo or a crocodile. When we scan through all land-dwelling creatures—both living and extinct— which one comes up as the "first in rank," the most colossal or the chief? Clearly the sauropod dinosaur. Pairing God's Word that Behemoth is the grandest creature He ever made with the fact that sauropods are the largest land creatures we've ever found should give us a clue to Behemoth's identity.

Sauropods were huge. The largest one found to date (named *Patagotitan mayorum*) was over 120 feet long—that's 10 freeway lanes across! At a weight of 76 tons, it's a wonder these creatures could even walk! Let's start by looking at one of their unique design features: their long necks.

The necks of the sauropod dinosaurs were by far the longest of any animal, six times longer than that of the world record giraffe and five times longer than those of all other terrestrial animals.[63]

Mamenchisaurus youngi
(Pi et al, 1996)

Figure 12. *Mamenchisaurus* a Type of Sauropod Dinosaur.[64]

The engineering required for a living creature to have such a long neck has perplexed dinosaur researchers for years—the physics just don't seem to work because the necks would be too heavy for their length. Leading sauropod researcher, Dr. Matthew Wedel notes: "They were marvels of biological engineering, and that efficiency of design is especially evident in their vertebrae, the bones that make up the backbone."[65] After spending years studying the long necks of sauropods, Dr. Wedel made a discovery that was so significant it earned him the Fourth International Award in Paleontology Research. In short, Dr. Wedel revealed that the vertebrae of these massive sauropods were pneumatic—they were *filled with air*![66]

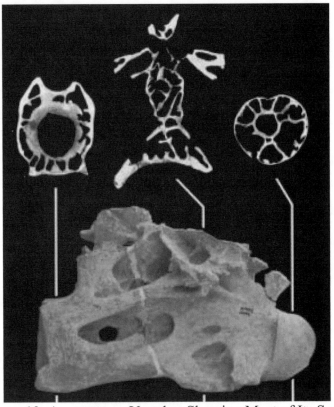

Figure 13. Apatosaurus Vertebra Showing Most of Its Space Filled with Air Cavities.[67]

Dr. Wedel started researching these air-filled vertebrae as an undergraduate researcher in Oklahoma, where he spent his Saturdays running dinosaur bones through the CT scanner at his local hospital. There, he discovered that "one of Sauropod's four and a half foot vertebrae would have been surprisingly light and could reach 90% air by volume!"[68]

Figure 14. A 4-1/2-Foot Sauropod Vertebra That Could Reach 90% Air by Volume.

More exhaustive studies by Dr. Wedel and others have revealed that the vertebrae of most sauropods were often 50–60% air by volume, with some as high as 90% (see Figure 14).[69] While Dr. Wedel estimates that this would only reduce the overall weight of some of these creatures by 8–10%, most of the weight would be removed from the critical areas of the neck, where extra weight would have been challenging for the creature to lift its head, eat, or turn around.

Yet there's more—these big creatures needed *light* vertebrae to enable them to lift their heads—but these extra-long necks also needed to be *designed* in such a way that the animal could eat, drink, and move its head without its neck folding in half or pinching vital nerves or even the trachea (for breathing) or esophagus (for eating). Having an extra-light structure was only part of the solution.

Take a close-up look at the neck vertebrae of these creatures (shown in Figure 15). Do you notice the shape of the vertebrae, and how they have protruding bones that face the same direction?

Figure 15. Royal Terrell Museum (Author)

Each of these protruding structures served as anchoring points for the connective soft tissue that held the neck together. Dinosaur researchers have also tried to figure out how the tendons, ligaments, and muscles must have been assembled for this creature to have a stable neck system. They've even proposed several complex models that try to demonstrate how everything might have fit together (Figure 16).

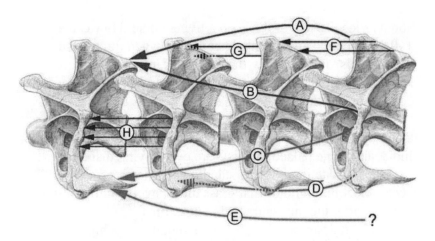

Figure 16. Sauropod Vertebrae (Taylor & Wedel, 2012).[70]

Taylor and Wedel developed a model showing what the connections that hold together the vertebrae might have looked like (Figure 16). The muscle passing behind the bone is shown using dashed lines; muscles inserting on the epiphyses (attachment areas for several neck muscles) are shown with lines C, D, E; muscles inserting on the cervical ribs are shown with lines F and G; and muscles inserting on the neural spine are shown with line H.

Does this look complicated? Yes, indeed—but that's only the *muscular* system. The *ligaments* and *tendons* still need to fit into the design in an amazing way for this creature to *swallow* and *breathe* through this complex neck system.

For this creature to eat, breathe, and move its long neck, the 12+ neck vertebrae[71] of sauropods had to be *interlocking* and *twistable*. Further, the vertebrae had to have anchoring points in *just the right places* for muscles and ligaments to connect in such a way to prevent the neck from pinching veins, nerves, trachea, and the esophagus.

While their air-charged vertebrae may solve the puzzle of how they could lift and move their massive heads and necks, it doesn't solve the challenge of how they could possibly inhale enough oxygen through their tiny nostrils, which were only about twice the size of those on a living horse! How can a 140,000+ pound animal inhale enough oxygen through such tiny nostrils? Perhaps they thrived better in a world before Noah's Flood when the oxygen levels were likely higher. We'll cover more on this topic later.

God even describes Behemoth's diet: eating grass like an ox. In 2005 researchers found grass in sauropod coprolites in India, and some palaeobotanists are even saying that this will cause a "rewrite in our understanding of dinosaur evolution," because evolution holds that grass didn't evolve until millions of years after the dinosaurs had gone extinct.[72]

God describes Behemoth's strength in his hips, and power in his stomach muscles. Again, we have a strong clue that Behemoth was a sauropod dinosaur because, while many animals have strong hips and stomach muscles, none were as strong as the sauropod! The muscular structure around the hips and stomach that were necessary for sauropods to move, walk, turn, and eat would be incredible! In fact, for some sauropods, like the Diplodocus, its highest point of its core body was the hips and its whole body balanced on the hips, front-to-back. Diplodocus was able to rear up on its back legs and balance on its tail like a tripod, making use of the hips to support not just the back half of its body, but the front half, too. This required enormous strength in the hip and stomach muscles, considering they lifted tons of its own body into the air. Below the hips was an incredible weight distribution system that went from a massive femur (which in some cases was nearly 8 feet long), to two shin bones, then five foot bones, and then five toes.

Behemoth's tail also closely matched those of sauropods. God describes that he "moves his tail like a cedar tree" and follows this by stating, "the sinews of his thighs are tightly knit." Paleontologists have learned from the muscle attachment locations in their bones that the tightly-knit structure of Behemoth's thighs and hips actually made his tail sway from side-to-side with each step, much as a cedar tree does when it sways in the wind![73] Tail drag marks are only rarely found behind sauropod footprints, indicating their tails were raised while they walked. It's difficult to think of a creature that fits this Biblical description better than a sauropod dinosaur.

God describes his bones "like beams of bronze." Most Bible versions translate this phrase as "tubes of bronze," "conduits of bronze," or "pipes of brass," which conveys both "strength" and being hollow like a channel or a tube. This matches the fact that that sauropods had the largest leg bones of any animal, and they are in fact just like tubes of metal, having a hard outer casing and spongy marrow and veins on the inside.

Then God says that its "ribs are like bars of iron." Unlike much of the sauropod's skeleton that was spongy and filled with air for weight savings, its ribs were *fully ossified*— they were made of solid bone![74] Again, there is a perfect match between God's description of Behemoth and a sauropod dinosaur.

God even describes Behemoth's habitat: "He lies under the lotus trees, in a covert of reeds and marsh. The lotus trees cover him with their shade" and "The willows by the brook surround him." This was a creature that had to be near lots of green food—living in a lush, tropical environment. Large sauropods had to eat a half a ton of vegetation every day, and they likely had to eat all day long to consume this amount of food.

Next God says: "Indeed the river may rage, yet he is not disturbed; He is confident, though the Jordan gushes into his mouth." Why would God point out that this animal can stand in a rushing river? Lots of animals can do this, depending on the size of the rushing river. In this case, God said, "the river may *rage*, yet he is *not disturbed*" and that Behemoth is confident even though this raging river should gush into his mouth. The Jordan river is the largest river in Palestine and it currently flows at only 15% of the rate it flowed in the past.[75] Even so, in the winter this river would be incredibly difficult to cross, and it would take a *very* sizable animal to stand *undisturbed* in the rushing current and, even more, let the current gush into its mouth! Some of the larger sauropods stood over 20 feet at the shoulders and weighed over 70 tons. Creatures of this size and mass could withstand a raging river better than any others.

Even with all this evidence, some say that Behemoth was a just a mythical creature. Why would God try to display His awesome creative power by describing something that never existed? Anyone can do that. And why would God say that Behemoth was the "chief" of all His creations after describing 13 real, still-living animals in the same passage? Why go through all the trouble to describe Behemoth as a grass-eating animal that lies peacefully in the shadow of the river plants along with his physical description, diet, and habitat—all of which happen to fit a known creature: a sauropod dinosaur?

Certain Bible footnotes[76] state that Behemoth was a hippo, elephant, or crocodile but these do not come close to matching all 14 characteristics God used to describe Behemoth. They certainly are not the "first in rank" or "chief" of God's creations. Would God tell Job to "gird up his loins" to behold the "chief of his creations" just to show off a hippo? An elephant? These creatures were plentiful! They also don't have tails that sway like cedar trees, and both of these animals have been captured and killed by man throughout history.

Table 8 lists 14 characteristics of this creature that are provided in Job 40, and a sauropod dinosaur seems to fit the description better than any other creature, alive or extinct.

Table 8. Behemoth Description from Job 40

Behemoth Description (Job 40)	Sauropod	Hippo	Crocodile
1 - "made along with" man	YES	YES	YES
2 - eats grass like an ox	YES	YES	NO
3 - strength in hips/stomach muscles	YES	NO	NO
4 - he moves his tail like a cedar	YES	NO	NO
5 - sinews of his thighs are tightly knit	YES	YES	YES
6 - bones are like beams of bronze	YES	NO	NO
7 - ribs like bars of iron	YES	MAYBE	MAYBE
8 - "chief/first" in rank of all God's creations	YES	NO	NO
9 - mountains yield food for him, and all the beasts of the field play there	YES	MAYBE	NO
10 - lies under lotus trees, in reeds/marsh	YES	NO	NO
11 - lotus trees cover him with their shade; willows by the brook surround him	YES	YES	YES
12 - The river may rage, yet he is not disturbed	YES	NO	NO
13 - He is confident, though the Jordan gushes into his mouth	YES	MAYBE	MAYBE
14 - unapproachable by anyone but its maker	YES	NO	NO

God says that only Behemoth's Creator can approach him, that he cannot be captured by humans when he is on watch, and that no one can use barbs to pierce his nose. These impossibilities fit sauropod dinosaurs better than other animals because of their towering heads and huge size. With a head that reached over 40 feet high, it could see people coming from far away. Its massive tail also makes him unapproachable. Based on what we know from fossils, some sauropods could cover a 200-foot circle with deadly force using their tails which could be over 50-feet long and weigh over 13,000 pounds.[77] Studies have shown that some sauropods could probably create sonic booms with their tails—just like a whip.[78]

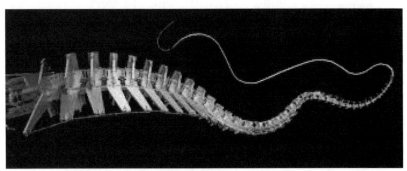

Figure 17. Study Demonstrated that Sauropod Tails Could Create Sonic Booms (D. Sivam / P. Currie / N. Myhrvold)

Figure 18. Behemoth's Tail Was One Reason Behemoth Was Unapproachable by Anyone but God, His Creator [79]

It's not by chance that God says to Job that Behemoth can *only be approached by his creator*. Good luck even getting near this creature to put a snare in its nose. To this day, elephants and hippos are surrounded by hunters and killed, but sauropods better fit this passage because they are simply unapproachable.

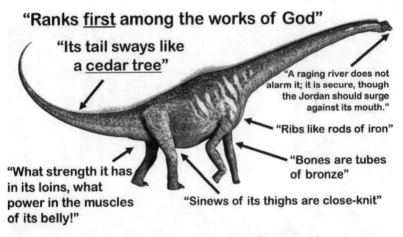

"Ranks <u>first</u> among the works of God"

"Its tail sways like a <u>cedar tree</u>"

"A raging river does not alarm it; it is secure, though the Jordan should surge against its mouth."

"Ribs like rods of iron"

"What strength it has in its loins, what power in the muscles of its belly!"

"Bones are tubes of bronze"

"Sinews of its thighs are close-knit"

Figure 19. Behemoth in Job Chapter 40.

This section has reviewed the incredible design features that all need to be present for these creatures to live. And the fact that these features—weight-bearing hips, legs, feet, and toes, incredible air-filled vertebrae, and others—show up already formed in the ~300 sauropods that have been found! Yes, there is variability within the sauropod kind, but these animals have been grouped by these (and other) common design characteristics. If God Himself created these animals and placed them on the Earth, then no wonder they had every aspect of their essential design features already in place and fully integrated from the start. The next dinosaur evidence that fits the Bible reviews the fossils.

Evidence #2: Lack of Dinosaur Ancestors and Transitions

The fact that secular dinosaur researchers cannot find the *ancestors* (from which the dinosaurs supposedly evolved) and the *transitions* between the different dinosaurs confirms the Biblical account that they were spontaneously placed here by God (each after their own *kind*—see Genesis 1:25). Figure 20 shows a reconstructed graphic from a leading dinosaur reference book: *The Encyclopedia of Dinosaurs.*[80]

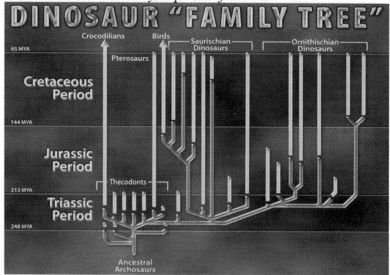

Figure 20. Dinosaur Ancestors and Transitions from *The Encyclopedia of Dinosaurs.*

In small print at the bottom of the chart in the *Encyclopedia of Dinosaurs* it states: "**Tinted areas indicate solid fossil evidence**" (these "tinted areas" are shown in Figure 20 by the broken lines above the tree that starts from the bottom, starting with "Ancestral Archosaurs"). Notice that fossil evidence only exists for the various kinds of dinosaurs themselves, with **no** precursors and **no** transitions! Indeed, the tree that starts at the bottom of the chart is a **theoretical** one because the "real data" based on actual dinosaur fossils only shows the different kinds of dinosaurs, that are always found after their own kind—just like the Bible says in Genesis 1:25: "God made the beasts of the Earth *after their kind...*"

Medical Doctor Carl Werner has done extensive research that confirms there are no ancestors or transitions for the dinosaurs. Dr. Werner spent 17 years traveling to the best museums and dig sites around the globe photographing thousands of original fossils and the actual fossil layers where they were found, and interviewing museum staff about this very question.

One of the examples of this is found in Dr. Werner's book, *Evolution: The Grand Experiment* where he provides a photo taken at the famous Chicago Field Museum. This museum display shows the theoretical evolution of dinosaurs, starting with the "common ancestor" and moving through the "transitions" covering a supposed time span of about 155 million years. There's just one major problem with this museum display—when inserting the number of dinosaur ancestors (at the beginning of the display) and the number of transitions at each of the branches, the display actually proves the *opposite* of what's intended. See Figure 21 that shows the display with these counts added.

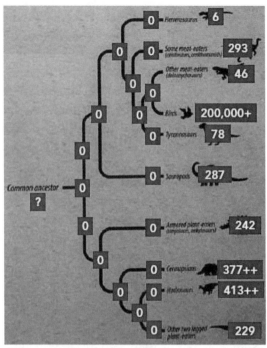

Figure 21. Dinosaur Evolution Display from the Chicago Field Museum (Counts Added).

After spending 17 years cataloging fossils at museums and interviewing hundreds of secular scientists about the fossil evidence of evolution, Dr. Werner found that they could not agree on a single common ancestor for all dinosaurs or any of the key supposed transitions between dinosaur kinds. Instead, each basic kind suddenly appeared on Earth. Notice that all the supposed transitions between the various dinosaur kinds have a 0 next to them. Dr. Werner could not find a *single* in-between transition that evolutionists can agree on. It's almost like someone just miraculously put dinosaurs here on Earth, each to reproduce after its own kind, just like the Bible says.

Dr. Werner explains the significance of Figure 21 by stating, "Over 30 million dinosaur bones have been discovered. Of these, thousands of individual dinosaur skeletons have been collected by museums representing over 700 dinosaur species.

Yet, not a single direct ancestor has been found for any dinosaur. Also, the proposed theoretical common ancestor for all dinosaurs has not been found."[81]

For example, Dr. Viohl, Curator of the Famous Jura Museum in Germany states the following about pterosaurs: "We know only little about the evolution of pterosaurs. The ancestors are not known... When the pterosaurs first appear in the geologic record, they were *completely perfect*. They were *perfect pterosaurs*"[82] (emphasis added). The same is true for every dinosaur group reflected on the chart.

If the theory of evolution is true, and one type of dinosaur evolved into another over millions of years, dinosaur evolution charts in textbooks around the world should be filled with numerous examples of dinosaur kinds evolving into others over the supposed 155 million years they were on Earth. But actual data shows the *exact* opposite.

Now that museums around the world have collected over 100,000 dinosaurs,[83] the number of "transitional" dinosaurs going between the various categories should be evenly distributed if evolution were true. But this is not the case. Even when interviewing numerous leading, evolution-believing scientists at these museums, Dr. Werner could not find a single scientist to offer any transitions. Instead, Dr. Werner found secular scientists stating the opposite. For example, Dr. David Weishampel, Editor of the encyclopedic reference book *The Dinosauria* wrote, "From my reading of the fossil record of dinosaurs, **no direct ancestors have been discovered for any dinosaur species**. Alas, my list of dinosaurian ancestors is an **empty** one." It appears that dinosaur evolution finds no basis in fossils.

Evidence #3: Dinosaur Anatomy Shows They Were Better-Suited for the Pre-Flood World

Biblical creationists and evolutionists both agree that the world in which dinosaurs lived was *different* than the world we live in today.[84] While we may not agree on *how* it was different

89

and *when* it was created and changed, we at least agree that Earth has not always been like it is today.

Volumes of evolutionary science papers and books have been written on the atmospheric conditions in which these massive and unusual dinosaurs existed. Some books, such as Peter Ward's *Out of Thin Air: Dinosaurs, Birds, and Earth's Ancient Atmosphere,*[85] have attempted to describe what this ancient world must have been like.

Ward, speaking from the evolutionary viewpoint, believes that changes in oxygen and carbon dioxide levels in the atmosphere over millions of years led to significant changes that allowed the expansion of different types of plants and animals. The basic idea is that the types of plants and animals that were suited for each period of Earth's changing condition survived, and those that were not died off.

Biblical Creation holds that God created a perfect initial world with no death, no carnivory, and no "survival of the fittest."[86] Further, animals were created to reproduce—just as we observe today—after their "own kind." Creationists also believe that this perfect world held out until it was marred by the sin of Adam and Eve, which brought death, suffering, bloodshed, and disease.[87] Geographically, this pre-Flood world had only a single landmass (Rodinia) until the Flood broke the continents apart less than 1,700 years after Creation.[88]

Biblical creationists have presented many pre-Flood climate models over the years, with many of them falling under the heading of "Canopy Models." While several variants exist, all canopy models interpret the "waters above" (firmament) in Genesis 1:7 to be some type of water-based canopy encircling the Earth that existed from the beginning of creation until the Flood. As scientific models, these ideas held promise to explain the pre-Flood climate, but they also produce many conditions (e.g., extreme surface temperatures) that make them problematic. While these models and others exist, we ultimately don't know what the pre-Flood world was like because we weren't there. Further, the Bible only gives a few insights to what the pre-Flood world was like:

- Before the Fall, the atmosphere was *perfect* for sustaining life in all ways (Genesis 1:31) and there was no death (Genesis 2:17; Romans 5:12; 1 Corinthians 15:22).
- Earth's atmosphere likely had sunlight and temperature variations within the days and nights (Genesis 3:8).
- Given that Adam and Eve were told to be "fruitful and multiply and fill the earth" (Genesis 1:27; 3:21) and they were "naked and unashamed" before the Fall (Genesis 2:25), it appears they had no need of clothing before the Fall.
- The Flood ruptured Rodinia and rearranged continents, creating extreme weather on the high mountains that were pushed up that the Flood elevated (Psalm 104:8).
- Genesis 2:5–6 states, "For the Lord God had not caused it to rain on the earth, and there was no man to till the ground; but a mist went up from the earth and watered the whole face of the ground." While some interpret this passage to mean that there was no rain until the Flood (a possibility), this passage is at least clear that before the Sixth Day of Creation Week, God had watered the plants with a mist and had not yet caused rain or created a man to till the ground.
- Because the rainbow was given to mark a new covenant between God and the Earth (to never again Flood the entire earth) (Genesis 9:13), there is the possibility that Earth's climate was changed after (and by) the Flood to allow rainbows.[89] However, God may have used an existing phenomena as a sign of His covenant.

These insights point to the idea that the pre-Flood world was quite different than the post-Flood world of today. The New Testament also acknowledges this distinction (2 Peter 3:6: "by which the world that then existed perished, being flooded with water"). Next let's turn to some clues in the fossil record that may also indicate that the pre-Flood world wasn't like today's world.

- Giant land beasts, such as sauropod dinosaurs that grew as large as 115 feet and 200,000 pounds.
- Giant flying reptiles, pterosaurs, with over 50-foot wingspans (e.g., *Quetzalcoatlus*).
- Giant dragonflies with 2-1/2 foot wingspans and 17-inch bodies (*Meganeura*).
- Mushrooms that grew over 20-feet high (*Prototaxites*).[90]
- Giant millipedes that grew over eight feet long (*Arthropleura*).

The above list could be much longer; these are just a few examples. Biblical creationists and evolutionists agree that these giant creatures and plants existed. Indeed, they are in the fossil record for everyone to evaluate, regardless of the worldview lens through which they are viewed. We also agree that these giant creatures and plants existed in a *different version of the Earth*, with evolutionists placing this version millions of years ago and Biblical creationists placing it before the Flood, about 4,400 years ago. Let's briefly review each of these examples.

Giant Land Beasts (Sauropods)

In the previous section, we looked at the massive, unmatched size of the sauropod dinosaurs, but we left out one important feature of this magnificent animal until now—*how they breathed*. Many who have studied this issue would agree that these creatures would have a difficult time staying alive very long in today's current atmosphere with only 21% oxygen levels. This is, at least in part, due to this animal's extremely small nasal passages compared to its enormous body size. See Figure 22.

"An 80-foot-long brontosaurus had a set of nostrils about the same size as a horse's... There were some serious problems with trying to get air into that animal."
– Richard Hengst, Purdue University Physiologist

Figure 22. Giant Sauropod[91]

Do you notice the immense size of the sauropod's body compared to its nasal passages? While the nasal structures of the different sauropods vary, one consistent trait is the extremely small nasal passages compared to their body size. The explanation given by some evolutionists is simply that the ancient Earth had higher oxygen levels (35%),[92] and when the oxygen level dropped, the dinosaurs died out (one of many dinosaur extinction theories offered by evolutionists).[93]

Scientists that have studied sauropod anatomy have recognized this challenge, stating: "An 80-foot-long brontosaurus had a set of nostrils about the same size as a horse's ... there were some serious problems with trying to get air into that animal. Dinosaurs could not have existed without having more oxygen in the air to start with."[94]

So just what were the oxygen levels of the pre-Flood world? To be fair, we really don't know. Some Biblical creationists have theorized, at least when it comes to giant insects that are in the fossil record that grew to enormous sizes, that oxygen levels might have played a part. For example, when discussing the fact that pre-Flood insects grew much larger than today and the possibility that higher oxygen levels may be one possible explanation, Drs. Carl Wieland and Jonathan Sarfati stated, "This may be because the pre-Flood world carried more oxygen-producing vegetation, possibly due to greater land area and 'floating forests,' much of it buried during the Flood." [95]

Giant Flying Reptiles (Pterosaurs)

One of the largest flying reptiles is *Quetzalcoatlus*, which was named after the Mesoamerican feathered serpent god, Quetzalcoatl. Many studies have attempted to estimate this creature's wingspan, with most estimates coming in over 36 feet.[96]

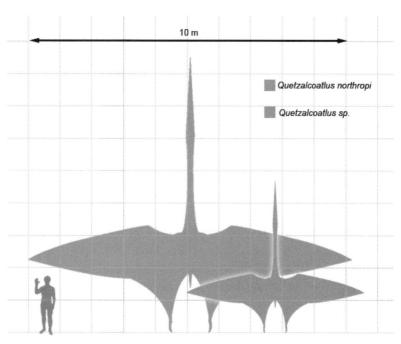

Figure 23. Quetzalcoatlus Wingspan[97]

The wingspan, however, is not what puzzles scientists about this giant—it's the *large wingspan given its weight.* While estimates vary, some studies estimate the weight of the larger specimens discovered to exceed 500 pounds.[98] That's likely too much weight for a flying creature to bear and still be able to fly. Several studies have investigated how these massive creatures could fly, with some reports even titled, "This Pterodactyl was so big it couldn't fly" and opening sentences such as "Bad news dragon riders: Your dragon can't take off."[99]

Scientists who have studied and published on this extensively have even admitted: "…it is now generally agreed that even the largest pterosaurs could not have flown in today's skies" and have offered explanations such as "warmer climate" or "higher levels of atmospheric oxygen" as reasons it could have flown only during the era in which it lived.[100]

Some secular studies that have investigated air bubbles trapped in amber that was dated to the "ancient world in which dinosaurs lived," have found *both* increased pressure as well as greater oxygen levels: "'One implication is that the atmospheric pressure of the Earth would have been much greater during the Cretaceous era, when the bubbles formed in the resin. A dense atmosphere could also explain how the ungainly pterosaur, with its stubby body and wing span of up to 11 meters, could have stayed airborne,' he said. 'The spread of angiosperms, flowering plants, during the Cretaceous era could have caused the high oxygen levels[101] reported by Berner and Landis.'"[102]

Interesting—giant sauropods couldn't likely breathe in today's world, giant flying reptiles that could not have flown in today's atmosphere—what's next? Giant dragonflies.

Giant Dragonflies (Meganeura)

The largest dragonfly species alive today (*Megaloprepus caerulatus*) has a wingspan of up to seven inches and a body up to five inches long. Based on the fossil record, the largest pre-Flood dragonflies (*Meganeura*) had wingspans up to 2-1/2 feet and a 17-inch body. See Figure 24.

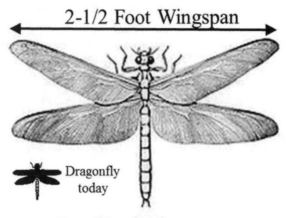

Figure 24. Giant Pre-Flood Dragonfly (*Meganeura*).[103]

In October 2006, *Science Daily* publicized a study led by Arizona State University staff titled "Giant Insects Might Reign if Only There Was More Oxygen in the Air."[104] The article claims:

> The delicate lady bug in your garden could be frighteningly large if only there was a greater concentration of oxygen in the air, a new study concludes. The study adds support to the theory that some insects were much larger during the late Paleozoic period because they had a much richer oxygen supply, said the study's lead

author Alexander Kaiser. The Paleozoic period…was a time of huge and abundant plant life and rather large insects—dragonflies had two-and-a-half-foot wing spans, for example. The air's oxygen content was 35% during this period, compared to the 21% we breathe now, Kaiser said.

This research lends evidence to the fact that the pre-Flood world was different than the one we live in today.

One study conducted in 2010 by researchers at Arizona State University tested this "more oxygen = bigger insects" theory directly by raising 12 different types of insects in simulated atmospheres with various oxygen levels. Their study included three sets of 75 dragonflies in atmospheres containing 12%, 21%, and 31% oxygen levels and their experiment confirmed that dragonflies grow bigger with more oxygen.[105] While there are likely a host of reasons why the pre-Flood dragonflies grew much larger than those today, especially genetic bottlenecking at the Genesis Flood, it is quite interesting to see the clear dichotomy between larger creatures of many types before the Flood compared to the animals alive today.

Giant Mushrooms (Prototaxites) and Plants

You don't need to read many secular-based books about the "ancient Earth" before learning about gigantic vegetation that existed supposedly millions of years ago. One example is the *Prototaxites* (see Figure 25). Some reports even state that these gigantic (now extinct) mushroom-like plants covered much of the Earth and "dotted the ancient landscape."[106]

Figure 25. *Prototaxites*

First discovered by a Canadian in 1859, no one seemed to know what they were. But after 130 years of debate whether this plant was a lichen, fungus, or some kind of tree, scientists have come to some level of agreement that it was essentially a "gigantic early mushroom."

Plants and fungi like these puzzle evolutionists, such as Kevin Boyce of Geophysical Sciences at University of Chicago, who stated, "A 20-foot tall fungus doesn't make any sense. Neither does a 20-foot tall algae make any sense, but here's the fossil."[107]

From a Biblical creationist standpoint, this is simply a gigantic pre-Flood fungus that was created to thrive in the pre-Flood world, but not now. In a temperate, pre-Flood world where wearing clothing was (originally) "optional," it's no wonder that giant fungus and plants like this could have thrived.

Giant Millipedes (Arthropleura)

Giant millipedes (called *Arthropleura*) that grew to be over eight feet long[108] used to crawl around before the Flood in what became northeastern America and Scotland. While evolutionists assign "millions of years" to these creatures, all we can know for total certainty is that they died. The larger species of this group are the largest known land invertebrates of all time. Evolutionists attribute their grand size to different pressures and/or oxygen levels of Earth's ancient past.[109]

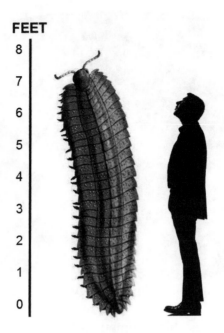

FEET

Figure 26. Giant Pre-Flood Millipedes (*Arthropleura*).

Evidence #4: The Vast Extent of the Fossil Record

President of Answers in Genesis, Ken Ham, has become well-known for making this statement: "If there really was a Global Flood, what would the evidence be? Billions of dead things, buried in rock layers, laid down by water all over the Earth." This is exactly what we see.

For example, the Paleobiology Database (PaleoBioDB) is a free, searchable database that is designed to "provide global, collection-based occurrence and taxonomic data for organisms of all geological ages."[110] This database includes 183,739 fossil *collections* totaling 1,323,009 *occurrences* (with each "occurrence" ranging from a few fossils to numerous). From a Biblical Creation standpoint, the Genesis Flood deposited the vast majority of these fossils. The circles in Figure 27 shows the extent of the known fossil record.

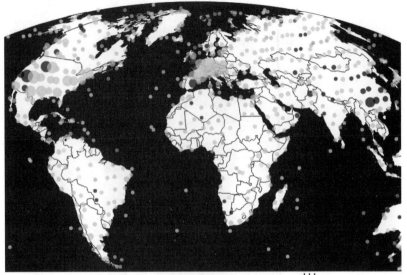

Figure 27. Paleobiology Database.[111]

If the untestable assumptions that hold up the ideas of radiometric dating are not true (and we believe they are not[112]), then Figure 27 displays a massive, watery graveyard, most of which was filled during the year-long Genesis Flood.

The number of dinosaur "mass graves" around the world is astounding. These fossil graveyards contain a mixture of many different kinds of fossils that have been *transported by large volumes of water* (see Figure 28). Modern, small-scale debris flows offer examples of what likely entrained in some cases millions of animals. Like a giant water wing, a debris flow carries its load largely undisturbed inside, as it rides upon a watery cushion either underwater or over land. As soon as the flow slows to a certain speed, turbulence overwhelms the load and it drops in place.

Figure 28. Fossil Graveyard Example.

Bone fossils typically occur as broken fragments. They were violently carried along with enormous mounds of mud and shifting sediments. By studying some of these fossil graveyards, we can gather clues that will demonstrate that the Flood was in fact catastrophic and worldwide, as stated in Genesis 7:20–23:

> The waters rose and covered the mountains to a depth of more than fifteen cubits [at least 22 feet]. *Every living thing* that moved on land perished—birds, livestock, wild animals, *all the creatures* that swarm over the earth, and *all mankind. Everything* on dry land that had the breath of life in its nostrils died. *Every living thing* on the face of the earth was wiped out; people and animals and the creatures that move along the ground and the birds were wiped from the earth. *Only Noah was left,* and those with him in the ark. (emphasis added)

If this passage in Genesis is true, we would expect to find *billions of dead things buried in rock layers laid down by water all over the earth.*[113] And this is exactly what we find *all over the world.*

Another profound example is Dinosaur National Monument in Utah, which is only a part of the 700,000-square mile Morrison Formation, a geologic unit that has spawned excavations of more than a hundred dinosaur quarries.[114]

Figure 29. Aerial extent of the Morrison Formation.[115]

What type of catastrophe could possibly bury hundreds of massive bone beds in this 700,000-square mile area, all at once? It could represent an enormous, ancient debris flow that only a worldwide watery catastrophe could reasonably explain.

Evidence #5: Dinosaurs Were Buried Furiously (Disarticulated)

Only about 3,000 of the dinosaur fossils that have been collected represent "articulated"[116] (bones still in place) animals. Because over 100,000 dinosaurs have been found, this represents only about 3% of the dinosaur fossil record.[117] So these animals did not die peacefully. Whatever wiped them out was *sudden* and *violent*.

I will never forget walking around at Dinosaur Provincial Park in Canada, which is one of the largest mass dinosaur graves in the world. In just this one area, over 32,000 fossil specimens have been found, representing 35 species, 34 genera, and 12 families of dinosaurs. Astonishingly, dinosaur fossils intermingle with fish, turtles, marsupial and other mammals, and amphibians. Also, only 300 complete animals have been found! The large majority were scrambled, pulverized, and blended together, as if the world became an enormous washing machine.

While walking around the outdoor exhibits, one display caught my daughter's eye. It was a large hadrosaur, a "duck-bill" dinosaur, that they left in the ground, exactly as it was found, covered with mud and twisted around like it went through a blender before it was buried. A young boy pushed a button to play the audio explanation provided by the museum that described the evolutionary idea about how the animal died. Their explanation was that a large tropical storm caused the rivers to rise and the dinosaurs to drown—one after the other— as each blindly followed the other to their death (thousands of them).[118]

This is when my daughter had her epiphany: "You've got to be kidding me!" she exclaimed. "Look at all these dead dinosaurs—they're everywhere! And they're buried in countless tons of sediment—how's a local rainstorm going to do that? Noah's Flood is a much better explanation!" She's onto something. If rainstorms explain this, then why don't they deposit and fossilize even smaller creatures today? This dinosaur graveyard was massive—spanning a 2.3 square kilometer area. Imagine walking around an area this size with thousands of buried Centrosaurs (estimates exceed 10,000 Centrosaurs alone!).[119] It was an eerie feeling!

Evidence #6: Dinosaurs Were Quickly Buried in Mud

The very fact that we have so many preserved dinosaur fossils shows that they were buried quickly because fossilization requires rapid burial in muddy ground. The fossil record is full of dinosaurs that suddenly died in watery graves around the world, with many of them found in the famous "death pose" with their necks arched back, as if drowning in mud.[120]

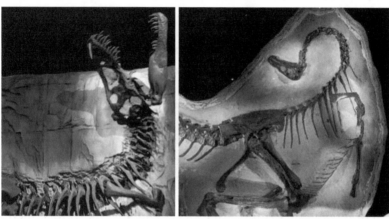

Figure 30. Dinosaurs in the Common "Death Pose," Indicating Rapid Burial and Suffocation (Royal Terrell Museum, Author).

Evidence #7: Dinosaurs Were Buried Simultaneously, Fleeing in Groups

Sauropod and Triceratops Graveyards

From a Biblical viewpoint, the Paleobiology Database is useful for finding where extinct animal groups (like dinosaurs) may have lived before they were wiped out by the Flood. For example, Figure 31 plots both the sauropod and triceratops dinosaur fossils that have been found in the Midwestern United States. Isn't it interesting that these totally different dinosaur types were simultaneously wiped out and buried in the *same areas*? Something stopped these two very large dinosaur types dead in their tracks and buried them in mud, preserving their fossils for us to find today.

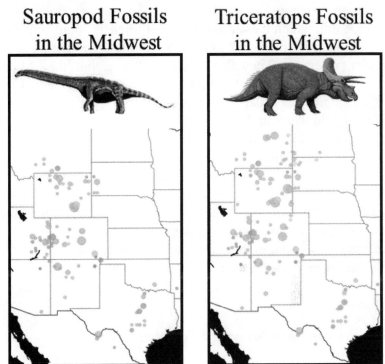

Figure 31. Sauropod and Triceratops Graveyards.

Sauropods and Triceratops are some of the largest dinosaurs to ever live. What type of event would it take to bury these massive creatures in mud so quickly that they would be disarticulated and preserved for us to find today—locked in mud that hardened into rock before getting scavenged? Slow, gradually-rising creeks or rivers? A sudden worldwide Flood explains more.

105

Thousands of Buried Centrosaurs in Hilda, Canada

The famous Hilda bone beds in Canada, briefly discussed above, actually include 14 dinosaur "bone beds" that contain thousands of buried Centrosaurs *found in the same stratigraphic column* (a term used in geology to describe the vertical location of rocks in a particular area). The authors who completed the most extensive study of the area described the sediment in which these dinosaurs are buried as "mudstone rich in organic matter deposited on the tract of land separating two ancient rivers."[121] They also concluded that each of the 14 bone beds was actually part of a single, massive "mega-bone bed" that occupied 2.3 square kilometers—almost a square mile! Stop and think about this for a minute. How did thousands of dinosaurs—of the same species—get herded up and simultaneously buried in mud?

These authors even concluded that the massive bone beds were formed when a herd of Centrosaurs *drowned during a flood*. These bone beds are also found with aquatic vertebrates such as fish, turtles, and crocodiles, showing that water was definitely involved in their transport and burial. In addition, almost no teeth marks indicated any scavenging after these animals died, probably because most of them died at the same time.[122]

Massive Dinosaur Graveyard Found in China

An online article on Discovery.com describes the dinosaur graveyard in China as the largest in the world, writing, "Researchers say they can't understand why so many animals gathered in what is today the city of Zhucheng to die." Thousands of dinosaur bones stack on top of each other in "incredible density," then they "suddenly vanished from the face of the earth."[123] Most of the bones are found within a single 980-foot-long ravine in the Chinese countryside, about 415 miles southeast of Beijing. Clearly, processes were going on in the past that were so violent they are hardly imaginable.

106

10,000+ Duck-billed Dinosaurs Buried Alive in Montana

In his article titled, "The Extinction of the Dinosaurs," Creation researcher and career meteorologist Michael Oard describes some of the numerous dinosaur graveyards that are found all over the world.[124] He believes this is solid evidence of Noah's worldwide Flood. Oard reported that one of the largest bone beds in the world is located in north-central Montana:

> Based on outcrops, an extrapolated estimate was made for 10,000 duckbill dinosaurs entombed in a thin layer measuring 2 km east-west and 0.5 km north-south. The bones are disarticulated and disassociated, and are orientated east-west. However, a few bones were standing upright, indicating some type of debris flow. Moreover, there are no young juveniles or babies in this bone-bed, and the bones are all from one species of dinosaur.

Two other scientists, Horner and Gorman, also described the bone bed: "How could any mud slide, no matter how catastrophic, have the force to take a two- or three-ton animal that had just died and smash it around so much that its femur— still embedded in the flesh of its thigh—split lengthwise?"[125] Oard concluded that a cataclysmic event is the best explanation for the arrangement of the bones.

Figure 32 shows the text from museum displays or articles about each particular dinosaur graveyard shown. Isn't it incredible that everyone admits that some type of watery catastrophe was responsible for piling up the dinosaurs into these mass graves?

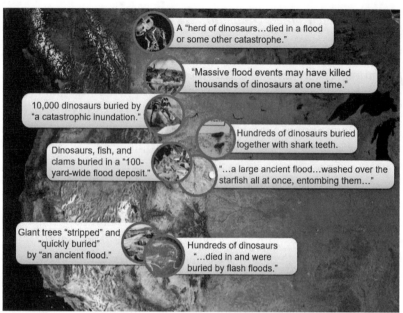

Figure 32. Dinosaur Graveyards in Midwestern United States, with "Flood Catastrophe" Explanations Even from Secular Sources.[126]

Evidence #8: Dinosaur Fossils Are Frequently Mixed with Marine Fossils

Mainstream scientists who deny that dinosaurs were buried in the Global Flood seem to closely clutch a "trade secret"—that dinosaur fossils are commonly found with marine fossils.[127] This is especially true of the Hell Creek Formation in Montana, where five shark species and 14 species of fish fossils have been found alongside dinosaurs.[128]

What in the world are shark and fish doing with massive land dinosaurs? Did a tropical storm pick up the sharks and fish and bury them with the dinosaurs? It seems that the Flood provides just about the only logical explanation. The Bible states in Genesis 7:11: "In the six hundredth year of Noah's life, in the second month, the seventeenth day of the month, the same day were *all the fountains of the great deep broken up, and the windows of heaven were opened.*" This describes a catastrophe of incomprehensible proportions. Breaking up *all the fountains of the deep* describes a mechanism that could cause massive, worldwide tsunamis that could carry ocean water far onto the continents, especially if the fountains of the deep included magma, and that magma repaved and elevated the world's ocean floors as geophysicist John Baumgardner has modeled.[129]

In addition to the Hell Creek area, this "mixing" of marine and land creatures is also evident in the Dinosaur Provincial Park in Canada where 12 families of dinosaurs are found mixed together with fish, turtles, marsupials, and amphibians. In Morocco, they've discovered sharks, sawfish, ray-finned fishes, and coelocanths in the same rock layers as a Spinosaurus dinosaur.[130]

Evidence #9: Dinosaurs Are Frequently Buried without Juveniles

Jack Horner, secular paleontologist, has spent a lifetime in the field hunting dinosaur fossils. In his book, *Digging Dinosaurs*, Horner reported one of the oddest findings of his career: The discovery of a huge dinosaur graveyard—over 10,000 adult Maiasaura in a small area, and yet no young were mixed in with them.[131]

What could have caused this odd sorting? If one adopts the Biblical Creation view, the Flood provides a very practical explanation. As Dr. Tim Clarey explains: "The adult dinosaurs were likely stampeding away from the imminent danger of raging floodwaters; their young could not keep up and became engulfed in some lower part of the peninsula."[132] This would explain Horner's maiasaurs, as well as the age-sorted deposits described above.

Evidence #10: Fresh Dinosaur Biomaterials[133]

Next, we'll take a look at 14 short-lived dinosaur biomaterials that remain in dinosaur bones and other body parts like skin and horns. Decay experiments have placed outer limits on how long they should last before completely decaying. For each of these materials, their "expiration date" is well before 65 million years, which is when dinosaurs supposedly went extinct. So, rather than being 65 million years old, these materials are just thousands of years old. The science of protein decay fits the Bible's timeline of dinosaurs recently buried in Noah's Flood.

Secular scientists have published each of these dinosaur-era fresh biomaterials in peer-reviewed evolution-based science journals. One of most frequently used "rescuing devices" that's given by evolutionists to try to explain some of these findings is "bacterial contamination." However, microbes do not produce *any* of the biomaterials covered below, ruling out recent contamination.

For readers who would like to dive deeper into this line of research, we recommend the Spring 2015 issue of the *Creation Research Society Quarterly Journal*,[134] which includes a technical review of what's covered in summary form below.

Fresh Dinosaur Biomaterial #1: Blood Vessels

Blood vessels transport blood throughout the body. They include the tiny capillaries, through which water and chemicals pass between blood and the tissue. Bones include capillaries and larger vessels. Small, pancake-shaped cells loaded with long-lasting collagen protein comprise blood vessels.

The blood vessels shown in Figure 33 were discovered when Dr. Mary Schweitzer's team was attempting to move a gigantic *Tyrannosaurus rex* fossil by helicopter that turned out to be too heavy. They were forced to break apart the leg bone. When looking at the inside of the leg bone at the lab, they discovered that the inside of the bone was partially hollow (not mineralized), revealing the soft tissue shown in Figure 33 that was extracted after treatments to remove the minerals.[135]

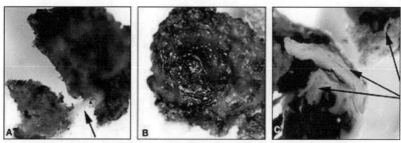

Figure 33. Tissue Fragments from a *Tyrannosaurus rex* Femur.[136]

The tissues that are shown on the left of Figure 33 show that it is flexible and resilient. When stretched, it returned to its original shape. The middle photo shows the bone after it was air dried. The photo at right shows regions of bone showing fibrous tissue, not normally seen in fossil bone.

Since this publication in 2005, blood vessels from several other dinosaurs and other extinct reptiles have been described and published in numerous leading scientific journals, including the *Annals of Anatomy*, *Science* (the leading journal of the American Association for the Advancement of Science), *Public Library of Sciences ONE*, and the *Proceedings from the Royal Society B*, which focuses on the biological sciences.[137]

Fresh Dinosaur Biomaterial #2: Red Blood Cells

Red blood cells carry oxygen and collect carbon dioxide using hemoglobin protein—also found in dinosaur and other fossils. Dr. Mary Schweitzer was one of the first to discover and publish the discovery of red blood cells, which she shares in her own words: "The lab filled with murmurs of amazement, for I had focused on something inside the vessels that none of us had ever noticed before: tiny round objects, translucent red with a dark center. Then a colleague took one look at them and shouted, 'You've got red blood cells. You've got red blood cells!'"[138]

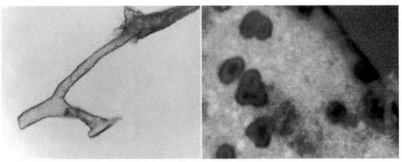

Figure 34. Red Blood Vessels and Cells from a *Tyrannosaurus rex* Bone.

These two photos in Figure 34 are from a 2005 discovery from Dr. Schweitzer that clearly show blood vessels from a *T. rex* bone (left) and red blood cells (right). How could these cells last for 65 million years? At least five peer-reviewed scientific journals have published accounts of red blood cells in dinosaur and other fossil bones.[139]

Regarding this discovery, Dr. Schweitzer remarked, "If you take a blood sample, and you stick it on a shelf, you have nothing recognizable in about a week. So why would there be anything left in dinosaurs?"[140] That's certainly a good question, and one that has an easier answer if dinosaurs are only thousands of years old!

After this discovery, Dr. Schweitzer ran into challenges when trying to publish her work in the scientific literature. Dr. Schweitzer remarks, "I had one reviewer tell me that he didn't care what the data said, he knew that what I was finding wasn't possible." Dr. Schweitzer wrote him back and asked, "Well, what type of data would convince you." The reviewer replied, "None."

Fresh Dinosaur Biomaterial #3: Hemoglobin

Hemoglobin protein contains iron and transports oxygen in red blood cells of most vertebrates. Some invertebrates, including certain insects and some worms, also use hemoglobin. In vertebrates, this amazing protein picks up oxygen from lungs or gills and carries it to the rest of the body's cells. There, oxygen fuels aerobic respiration by which cells produce energy.

Scientific studies have reported "striking evidence for the presence of hemoglobin derived peptides in the (T-rex) bone extract"[141] and several other dinosaur "era" bones.[142]

Fresh Dinosaur Biomaterial #4: Bone Cells (Osteocytes)

Secular scientists have described dinosaur proteins like hemoglobin, even though no experimental evidence supports the possibility that they can last for even a million years. But dinosaur bones hold more than just individual proteins. They sometimes retain whole cells and tissue remnants. An osteocyte is a bone cell that can live as long as the organism itself. Osteocytes constantly rebuild bones and regulate bone mass. Figure 35 shows highly magnified blood vessels, blood products, and osteocytes that were found on the inside of a brow horn of a Triceratops.

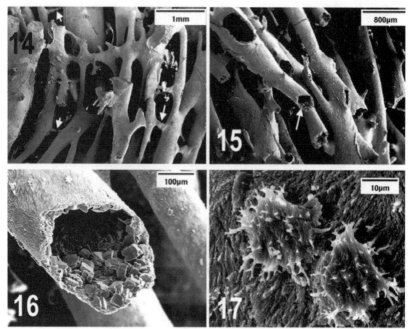

Figure 35. Soft Bone Material from a Brow Horn of a
Triceratops horridus from Montana.[143]

Figure 35 shows blood vessels linked together (white
arrows in frame 14). Frame 15 shows possible blood products
lining inner wall of hardened vessel (white arrow). Frame 16 is
enlarged from frame 15 and shows crystallized nature of
possible blood products lining inner wall of hardened vessel.
Frame 17 shows two large oblate osteocytes lying on fibrillar
bone matrix.

At least four scientific studies have established
osteocytes in dinosaur bones. One study even found nucleic
acid signatures consistent with ancient DNA right where the
nucleus would have been in dinosaur osteocytes.[144]

Fresh Dinosaur Biomaterial #5: Ovalbumin (Proteins)

Another protein found in fossils that microbes don't
make is called ovalbumin. It makes up 60–65% of the total

protein in egg whites. Ovalbumin has been found in exceptionally preserved sauropod eggs discovered in Patagonia, Argentina, a dig site that included skeletal remains and soft tissues of embryonic titanosaurid dinosaurs. These findings were reported in a peer-reviewed scientific journal.[145]

Fresh Dinosaur Biomaterial #6: Chitin

Chitin is a biochemical found in squid beaks and pens, arthropod exoskeletons, and certain fungi. If chitin was meant to last for millions of years, then it might have filled Earth's surface as dead insects, krill, and fungi left their remains over eons. Chitin is tough, but no known experiment supplies any reason to so much as suspect that it could last a million years, let alone hundreds of millions, as at least two scientific studies report finding in fossils.[146] Our Creator equipped many microbes with unique enzymes that digest chitin, so what could have kept those microbes away from all that chitin for millions of years?

Fresh Dinosaur Biomaterial #7: Unmineralized Bone

Fresh-looking, un-mineralized dinosaur bones pop up in dig sites around the world. In Alaska, for example, a petroleum geologist working for Shell Oil Company discovered well-preserved bones in Alaska along the Colville River. The bones looked so fresh that he assumed these were recently deposited, perhaps belonging to a mammoth or bison. Twenty years later scientists recognized them as Edmontosaurus bones—a duck-billed dinosaur.[147]

Figure 36. Unfossilized Hadrosaur Bone from the Liscomb Bone Bed.[148]

Mineralized bones can look darker than bone and typically feel quite heavy. Un-mineralized bones retain their original structure, often including the tiny pore spaces in spongy bone, as shown in Figure 36. One study includes an interesting section that states:

> Finally, a two-part mechanism, involving first cross-linking of molecular components and subsequent mineralization, is proposed to explain the surprising presence of still-soft elements in fossil bone. These results suggest that present models of fossilization processes may be incomplete and that *soft tissue elements may be more commonly preserved, even in older specimens, than previously thought.*[149]
> Additionally, in many cases, osteocytes with defined nuclei are preserved, and may represent

an important source for informative molecular data (emphasis added).

Numerous other studies published in scientific journals have described these un-mineralized dinosaur bone findings.[150] Sometimes evolutionists are surprised by the fact that many dinosaur bones contain "fresh," original bone. It seems that decades of conditioning that "dinosaur bones become solid rocks" and ideas of "millions of years" have framed assumptions that are frequently being broken today.

However, researchers out in the field—actually digging bones—oftentimes have a different viewpoint. Take Dr. Mary Schweitzer's testimony for example, where she notes that many "fresh" dinosaur bones still have the stench of death:

> This shifting perspective clicked with Schweitzer's intuitions that dinosaur remains were more than chunks of stone. Once, when she was working with a *T. rex* skeleton harvested from Hell Creek, she noticed that the fossil exuded a distinctly organic odor. "It smelled just like one of the cadavers we had in the lab who had been treated with chemotherapy before he died," she says. Given the conventional wisdom that such fossils were made up entirely of minerals, Schweitzer was anxious when mentioning this to Horner [a leading paleontologist]. "But he said, 'Oh, yeah, all Hell Creek bones smell,'" she says. To most old-line paleontologists, the smell of death didn't even register. To Schweitzer, it meant that traces of life might still cling to those bones.[151]

Experienced dinosaur fossil collectors have developed similar opinions. Take experienced dinosaur hunter and wholesaler, Alan Stout, for example. Alan Stout is a long-time fossil collector and has collected and sold millions of dollars' worth of dinosaur specimens to collectors, researchers, and museums worldwide.[152] After collecting in the Montana Hell Creek formation (and surrounding areas) for over a decade Alan states that many of the dinosaur bones he finds in the Cretaceous layers are only 40% mineralized, with as much as 60% of the bone being original material. He even notes that some of the fossils "look just like they were buried yesterday after scraping off just the outside layer of mineralization."[153]

Fresh Dinosaur Biomaterial #8: Collagen

Collagen is the main structural protein found in animal connective tissue. When boiled, collagen turns into gelatin, showing its sensitivity to temperature. In 2007, scientists discovered collagen amino acid sequences from a *T. rex* fossil that supposedly dated at 68 million years. Met with controversy, some suggested these proteins came from lab workers who accidentally contaminated the samples being studied. Or perhaps traces of ostrich bone proteins lingered in the equipment used in the study. Some even said, well perhaps "a bird died on top of the *T. rex* excavation site."[154] However, three separate labs verified collagen in dinosaurs in 2009[155] and again in January 2017.[156] The 2017 study even confirmed the collagen at the *molecular level*, and stated, "We are confident that the results we obtained are not contamination and that this collagen is original to the specimen."[157]

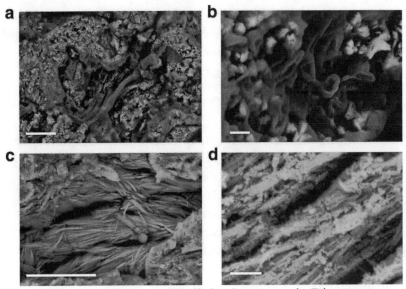

Figure 37. Fibers and Cellular Structures in Dinosaur Specimens.[158]

Experiments have projected that the absolute theoretical maximum life of collagen ranges from 300,000 to 900,000 years under the best possible conditions.[159] This shows that collagen proteins should not last one million years, but could (in the absence of microbes) last for thousands of years. This confronts millions-of-years age assignments for dinosaur remains, but is consistent with the biblical time frame.

But the "rescuing devices" being offered by evolutionists are not far behind. For example, in a recent article published in *Science*, Dr. Schweitzer tried to explain how the collagen sequences supposedly survived tens of millions of years: "... as red blood cells decay after an animal dies, iron liberated from their hemoglobin may react with nearby proteins, linking them together. This crosslinking, she says, causes proteins to precipitate out of solution, drying them out in a way that helps preserve them." Critical of this idea, however, Dr. Matthew Collins, a paleoproteomics expert at the University of York in the United Kingdom, stated that he doesn't think that the process described by Dr. Schweitzer could "arrest protein degradation for tens of millions of years, so he, for one, remains skeptical of Schweitzer's claim: 'Proteins decay in an orderly fashion. We can slow it down, but not by a lot.'"[160]

Fresh Dinosaur Biomaterial #9: DNA (Limited)

One measured decay rate of DNA, extracted from recently deposited fossil bird bones, showed a half-life of 521 years. DNA decays quickly. It should have spontaneously decayed into smaller chemicals after several tens of thousands of years—and it could only last that long if kept cool. A few brave secular scientists have reported DNA structures from dinosaur bones, although they did not directly address the question of its age.[161]

Fresh Dinosaur Biomaterial #10: Skin Pigments

In 2008, a group of paleontologists found exceptionally well-preserved Psittacosaurus remains in China and published images of dinosaur collagen fiber bundles. Other scientists published stunning skin color images from a separate Psittacosaurus, also from China, and found evidence of original, unaltered pigments including carotenoids and melanins. Nobody has performed an experiment that so much as suggests these pigments could last a million years. Still other studies have reported scale skin and hemoglobin decay products—still colored red as were some of Dr. Mary Schweitzer's *T. rex* and hadrosaurine samples—in a Kansas mosasaur.[162]

Fresh Dinosaur Biomaterial #11: PHEX (Proteins)

PHEX is a protein involved in bone mineralization in mammals. In 2013, Dr. Mary Schweitzer published detailed findings of the soft, transparent microstructures her team found in dinosaur bones. Because this discovery was so controversial, her team used advanced mass spectrometry techniques to sequence the collagen. Other methods demonstrated that proteins such as Actin, Tubulin, and PHEX found in osteocytes from two different dinosaurs were not from some form of contamination, but came from the creatures' remains.[163]

Fresh Dinosaur Biomaterial #12: Histone H4 (Proteins)

Bacteria do not make histone H4, but animals do. DNA wraps around it like a spool. Dr. Mary Schweitzer and her team found this protein inside a hadrosaur femur found in the Hell Creek Formation in Montana, which bears an assigned age of 67 million years. It might last for thousands of years if kept sterile, but no evidence so much as hints that it could last for a million years.[164]

Fresh Dinosaur Biomaterial #13: Keratin (Structural Protein)

Keratin forms the main structural constituent of hair, feathers, hoofs, claws, and horns. Some modern lizard skins contain tiny disks of keratin embedded in their scales. Researchers identified keratin protein in fossilized lizard skin scales from the Green River Formation that supposedly date to 50 million years ago. They explained its presence with a story about clay minerals attaching to the keratin to hold it in place for all that time. However, water would have to deposit the clay, and water helps rapidly degrade keratin. The most scientifically responsible explanation should be the simplest one—that this fossil is thousands, not millions of years old.[165] Other fossils with original keratin include Archaeopteryx[166] bird feather residue and stegosaur spikes.[167]

Fresh Dinosaur Biomaterial #14: Elastin

Elastin is a highly elastic protein found in connective tissue, skin, and bones. It helps body parts resume their shape after stretching or contracting, like when skin gets poked or pinched. Bacteria don't need it or make it, and elastin should not last a million years, even under the best preservation environment. Scientists reported finding this protein in a hadrosaur femur found in the Hell Creek Formation in Montana.[168]

Biomaterial Summary

Because these findings are game-changers, they are not without challenge by those who hold strongly to evolutionary ideas. Some of the "rescuing devices" that have been offered to attempt to explain these findings include iron in the blood acting as a preservative, the material being mistaken from a bird carcass mixed with the fossil, laboratory contamination, and even microbial biofilm (from bacteria in the bones). These explanations show an eagerness to attempt to dismiss the findings while clinging to the belief in millions of years. Rather than questioning the supposed long ages needed to prop up the evolutionary view, they seek other explanations to explain the presence of these materials.

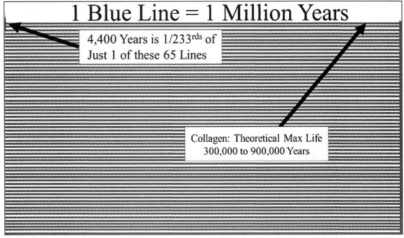

Figure 38. Dinosaur Biomaterials Time Comparison.

Figure 38 shows a simulated timeline to attempt to put these findings into perspective. Each of these 65 lines represents

1 million years. Showing 4,400 years on this chart is difficult, but is represented by a tiny dot in the upper left, which is 1/233rds of just one of these lines, or less than one-half of 1 percent of one of these lines. While this assumption can never be tested, some studies have measured an absolute theoretical maximum life of between 300,000 and 900,000 years.[169] If these dinosaur bones are really 65 million years old (and older), this collagen lasted for *72 to 217 times longer than these measured and extrapolated maximum collagen shelf lives.* Does this require strong faith?

Is it really possible that all 14 of these biomaterials lasted for 65 million years? If they represent more recent deposits and were quickly sealed in Noah's Flood only thousands of years ago, then these finds fit fine. The fact that these materials lasted even this long is remarkable, but within measured age estimates. These 14 fresh biomaterials—along with carbon-14 as we'll see next—clearly fit a timescale of just thousands of years more accurately than millions of years.

Evidence #11: Carbon-14 Found in Dinosaur Bones

Secular scientists typically don't look for carbon-14 in dinosaur bones because evolutionary deep time does not allow the possibility of recently-deposited dinosaurs. Carbon-14 decays so fast that all of it would spontaneously turn into nitrogen 14 in fewer than 100,000 years. According to evolutionists, why even look for it in samples that are supposed to be much older than this?

The Spring 2015 issue of the *Creation Research Society Quarterly Journal*[170] carried a study that tested seven dinosaur bones from Montana, Canada, and Oklahoma that five different laboratories detected carbon-14 in all samples from Cenozoic, Mesozoic, and Paleozoic source rocks. How did radiocarbon get there if it supposedly has a maximum shelf life of 100,000 years?

Several carbon-14 dating studies have shown the presence of carbon-14 in dinosaur bones and other fossils and

Earth materials. If dinosaur bones are 100,000 years—let alone 65 million years—old, not one atom of carbon-14 should remain in them. But both secular and creation scientists have now published findings of small amounts of carbon-14 from ancient wood, coal, fish bones, lizard bones, ammonites, clams, diamonds, oil, marble, and dinosaur bone. It's as if the whole Earth's surface is thousands, not millions, of years old. But that means the Bible's history is correct and that evolutionary history leans more on imagination than observation.

Evidence #12: Dinosaur Mummies

Charles Sternberg discovered the first dinosaur mummy in Wyoming in 1908. This duck-billed dinosaur (*Edmontosaurus annectens*) was one of the finest dinosaur specimens discovered (until replaced by "Leonardo"—see below). It was the first dinosaur find on record that included a skeleton encased in skin impressions from large parts of the body (see Figure 39).

Figure 39. The Trachodon Mummy on Exhibit in the American Museum of Natural History (2008).[171]

Dan Stephenson discovered "Leonardo" in 2000. This dinosaur mummy is one of the best-preserved dinosaur fossil in the world, which is about 90 percent covered in soft tissue, including skin, muscle, nail material, and a beak. Skin impressions have even been found on the underside of the skull and all along the neck, ribcage, legs, and left arm.[172] This finding was so well preserved it even made the *Guinness Book of World Records*.

Figure 40. Leonardo's Guinness World Record Certificate.

They even found the "fresh" content of Leonardo's last meal in his stomach! More than 40 different kinds of plants were found in his stomach and intestines, including tree leaves, flowers, ferns, shrubs and even algae that he likely swallowed getting a drink of water.[173] One must ask: How in the world did these soft tissues, leaves, flowers, and ferns last for over 77 million years? Seems very unlikely. Biblical creationists would place this animal about 4,400 years old, quickly buried by the Genesis Flood and sealed beneath sand for us to find today in

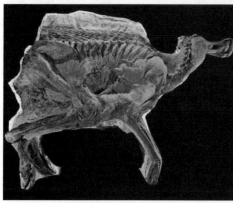
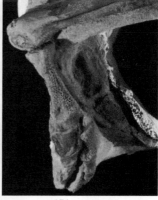

Figure 41. Leonardo Dinosaur Mummy[174] and Foot.

"fresh" condition. Comparing the two worldviews, 77 million years is about *18,000 times longer* than 4,400 years.

These types of finds do not surprise Biblical creationists. Rapidly-sealed animals can stay intact for thousands of years. But millions upon millions of years is another story!

Our discussion on collagen (above) provides some estimates on how soft tissues can possibly last thousands of years, but certainly not millions. Recently even a fossilized heart was found that supposedly dates to over 113 million old.[175] A fossilized dinosaur brain was also recently discovered, dating to 133 million years old using the evolutionary timescale.[176]

Figure 42. Fossilized Dinosaur Brain.[177]

Soft tissues disintegrate. They go back to the dust. Seeing how some soft tissues can in fact be preserved and last for thousands of years testifies to both the *recent* and *catastrophic nature* of the Flood.

Conclusion

We've reviewed 12 lines of evidence that seem to align more with biblical history than evolution-based theories. We started with how dinosaurs seem to be "cleverly designed" with features that shout "intention" and "intelligent design."

Dinosaur fossil evidence shows that when these creatures are found in the crust of the earth, they always show up completely formed, with incredible design. Transitional forms that are "leading" to dinosaurs are simply not found. The evidence points to a magnificent designer placing the creatures here, fully-formed, and ready to live and thrive in a pre-Flood paradise.

The vast fossil record indicates catastrophic burial, with the animals furiously buried in mud—found fleeing in groups—and sometimes without juveniles. The fact that many dinosaur mass graves are found mixed together with marine fossils points to only one logical conclusion: the oceans came quickly onto dry land, burying both land- and sea-creatures simultaneously. Some dinosaurs are even buried so fast that they are mummified and found complete with their last meals still in their stomachs.

Finally, we have at least 14 "fresh" biomaterials found in dinosaur bones, horns, and claws that—according to even secular science—cannot last for millions of years. Finding detectable levels of carbon-14 in their bones also confirms a timescale of thousands of years, not millions.

If the biblical narrative is correct about dinosaurs, and we believe that it is, then it's also likely correct about *everything else*.[178] After diving into this research years ago, this is exactly what I learned. It became clear to me that the dinosaur data fit the biblical framework better than the evolutionary one, and it fueled my faith even more, solidifying my understanding that the Bible is true both theologically *and* historically.

To Christians, these evidences should serve as a wake-up call. To those who aren't yet Christians, the evidences we've reviewed can be the start of a life-long journey leading to incredible things, both in this life, and the one to come.

Chapter 5: Ape Men?
Science Refutes Human Evolution

Reading through a 6th grade World History textbook might lead the reader to believe that there are thousands of examples of humanlike creatures that lead up to modern humans. **But do you know that you could fit all the bones that supposedly prove human evolution into a pickup truck?**[179]
According to Biblical Creation, God made Adam and Eve only about six thousand years ago, and all human varieties—living and extinct—descend from the original couple. According to evolution, death of "less fit" apes into humans over millions of years. We cannot rewind time to view firsthand the creation of mankind, but we have lots of evidence supporting creation. Unfortunately, school textbooks don't mention this evidence.
If the Bible is true, God created us supernaturally, a reason exists for our creation, and we will eventually answer to God for how we lived our lives. On the other hand, if public school textbooks are correct and natural processes made us, we have no lasting purpose, and will not be held accountable to a Creator after this life. Think about it—if you believe that humans evolved from apes, then why not just live like you want to live? Without a God, there is no "good," no "evil," and no basic moral laws like the Ten Commandments to guide your life. In this view, there would be no afterlife, no judgment, and no accountability after you die! However, if we believe in a God who made us on purpose, we have meaning, significance, and accountability in this life, and a hope for everlasting life. Knowing where we came from gives us a firm foundation for daily decisions and even everlasting decisions. This is not just a side issue. It impacts every area of our lives.

A Quick-Tour Through Human Evolution Icons

Key icons have carried the idea that humans evolved from ape-like creatures beginning millions of years ago. However, these iconic fossils fit categories like "extinct ape," "extinct human variety," and "hoax," but none of them fit the imaginary "ape-like ancestor" category. Let's briefly look at just three of the most famous icons that have been used over just this last century: Piltdown Man, Nebraska Man, and Neanderthals.

Piltdown Man

Piltdown Man was a main icon of human evolution from 1912 to 1953, over 40 years. He was even given the scientific name *Eoanthropus dawsoni*, and over 500 books[180] and papers were written about this icon. Then, in 1953, the truth came out that the whole thing was a fraud, being made of a doctored ape jaw and human skull, both artificially stained to look old.[181] Nonetheless, Piltdown Man received a lot of press, and was even credited by the New York Times as "proving" Darwin's Theory of Evolution! (see Figure 43)

The New York Times.

SUNDAY, DECEMBER 22, 1912.

DARWIN THEORY IS PROVED TRUE

English Scientists Say the Skull Found in Sussex Establishes Human Descent from Apes.

THOUGHT TO BE A WOMAN'S

Bones Illustrate a Stage of Evolution Which Has Only Been Imagined Before.

Figure 43. Piltdown Man Announced in the New York Times (1912).[182]

In 1915, Sir Arthur Keith, Conservator of the Royal Medical College in England and President of the Royal Anthropological Institute of Great Britain and Ireland in the early 1900s, wrote the most definitive human evolution text of that era, *The Antiquity of Man*.[183] This 500+ page book prominently displayed a gold embossed skull of the Piltdown Man.

Over 100 pages of Arthur Keith's *The Antiquity of Man* book[184] is devoted to Piltdown Man, which was revealed as a fraud just two years before Keith died in 1955.[185] Keith placed so much trust in Piltdown Man as a "proof of evolution" that he

130

called it: "one of the most remarkable discoveries of the twentieth century."[186] Boy was he wrong! But it was too late. He had convinced his readers that human evolution had scientific backing, when it never did.

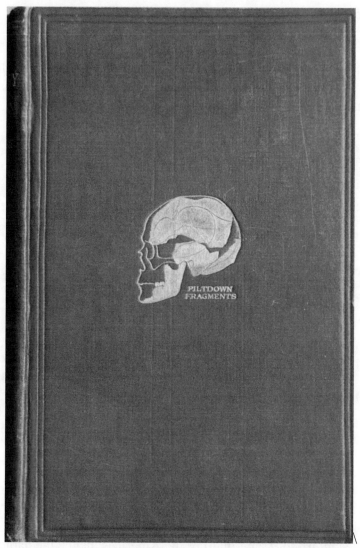

Figure 44. Sir Arthur Keith's Leading Human Evolution Book of the Early 1900s with Piltdown Man on the Cover.[187]

Historians continue to investigate who did it and why. A 2016 report showed evidence that Charles Dawson performed the forgery by himself. In any case, Piltdown Man was a hoax.[188]

Nebraska Man

From 1917 to 1928, yet another icon dominated the scene as "certain proof" of human evolution. Geologist Harold Cook found a ***single molar tooth*** in Nebraska which later was named *Hesperopithecus haroldcooki*, or Nebraska Man.

Figure 45. Nebraska Man[189]

In 1922, the head of the American Museum of Natural History (Henry Fairfield Osborn) proclaimed that the single molar found by Harold J. Cook in 1917 belonged to the first *pithecanthropoid* (ape-man) of the Americas, hence the name "western ape." The globally-distributed *Illustrated London News* broadcast British evolutionist Grafton Elliot Smith's receiving knighthood for his efforts in publicizing Nebraska Man. This imaginative "reconstruction" of the tooth's owner is a club-carrying ape-man walking upright. It shows primitive tools, possibly domesticated animals, and a brutish bride gathering roots. An artist derived all this from a single tooth! In July 1925, the Nebraska Man tooth was used to prove man evolved from ape-like creatures in the Scopes "Monkey Trial" held in Dayton, Tennessee.

This all changed when excavations continued in 1927–1928 at the same place the tooth was found. These excavations revealed that the tooth belonged neither to man nor ape, but to a wild pig![190] Then, in 1972, living herds of this same pig were discovered in Paraguay, South America.[191] According to the late renowned creation scientist Duane T. Gish, "this is a case in which a scientist made a man out of a pig, and then the pig made a monkey out of the scientist!"[192] "Nebraska man" turned out to be another hoax.

Neanderthals

Neanderthals were used to promote the idea of human evolution for over 120 years, and most people over 40 today will remember them widely used in textbooks as the ancient, half-ape, half-human brutes that "modern humans" supposedly evolved from. But over the last few decades, researchers have finally recognized fully human features in Neanderthal burials. They buried their dead, made musical instruments, tools, cosmetics, jewelry, and purses. Recent DNA sequence comparisons even confirm that they interbred with humans! While they had some differences in size and shape compared to people today, they were most certainly just people. Neanderthals represent extinct varieties of mankind, much in the same way that mammoths represent extinct varieties of the elephant kind.

Figures 46 and 47 show this changing position on Neanderthals—from pre-human "brute" to human.

Figure 46. Previous Idea of Neanderthal Man (published in *L'Illustration and in the Illustrated London News* in 1909).[193]

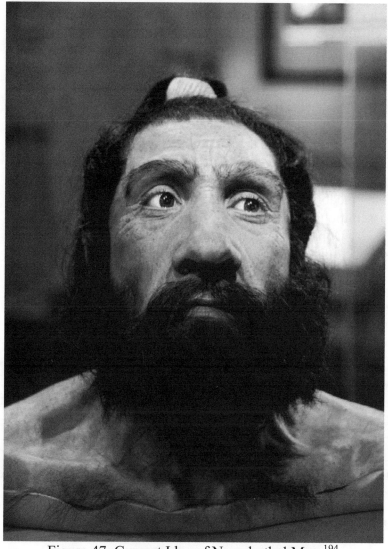

Figure 47. Current Idea of Neanderthal Man.[194]

Once considered an ape-like caveman, Neanderthal remains have proven their identity as fully human. Give him a shave, haircut, and button-down shirt and this Neanderthal would blend right into a city crowd.

Lucy: The Leading Human Evolution Icon of the 21st Century

See our Lucy Video: *www.genesisapologetics.com/lucy/*

Now we turn to the leading human evolutionary icon of today: Lucy. The year 1974 welcomed the famous "Lucy," a fossil form that bears the name *Australopithecus afarensis*. Lucy is arguably the most famous human evolution icon ever displayed in public school textbooks. Pictures and dioramas of Lucy inhabit countless museums and thousands of articles and dissertations.

Donald Johanson discovered Lucy in Ethiopia, Africa, and she quickly grew to be known as the supposed "missing link" between man and ape. At only about 3-1/2 feet tall and only about 60 pounds, she's very close to the size of small apes today.[195] The scientific name *Australopithecus* simply means "southern ape." Southern ape is a very appropriate name because, as you'll learn below, Lucy was just that—an ape!

Although public school textbooks often state that Lucy was our ancestor and they feature human-like drawings of her, the fossil evidence tells quite a different story. Over 40 years of Lucy research and about 20 more discoveries of her kind have raised new questions about its supposed evolutionary connection. Evolutionary research journals have substantiated ten fatal flaws regarding the claim that Lucy and her species are really our early ancestors.[196]

Fatal Flaw #1: Lucy's Skull

Even though only a few fragments of Lucy's skull were found, they revealed that her skull was about the same size as a chimpanzee. As Donald Johanson himself said, "Her skull was almost entirely missing. So knowing the exact size of Lucy's brain was the crucial bit of missing evidence. But from the few skull fragments we had, it looked surprisingly small."[197] Later estimates reveal that Lucy's brain was just one third the size of

136

a human brain, which makes Lucy's brain the same size as the average chimpanze brain.[198]

Sir Solly Zuckerman, chief scientific advisor to the British government, said that the "*Australopithecine* skull is in fact so overwhelmingly ape-like, as opposed to human that the contrary position could be equated to an assertion that black is white."[199]

The skull in Figure 48 shows a rendition of what Lucy's skull may have looked like. Notice that the brown parts are what they found; the white parts used to fill in most of the skull are imagined. Notice its sloped and ape-like. It's also the size and shape that closely resembles a modern bonobo (a cousin to the chimp).

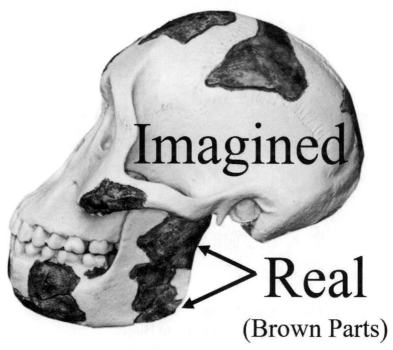

Figure 48. Lucy's Skull Reconstruction.[200]

Leading paleontologist, Dr. Leakey, stated, "Lucy's skull was so incomplete that most of it was 'imagination made of plaster of Paris,' thus making it impossible to draw any firm conclusion about what species she belonged to."

The Foramen Magnum

The foramen magnum is a hole in the bottom of a skull where the top of the spinal cord enters. The angle at which the spinal cord entered the foramen magnum of Lucy's species is nearly identical to a chimp's—indicating that Lucy's species walked hunched-over on all fours.[201]

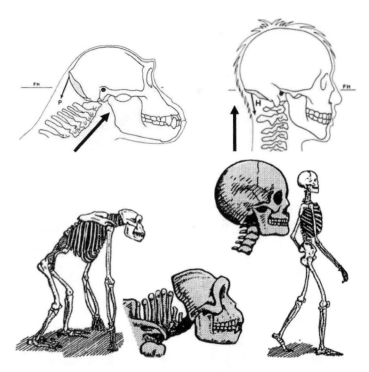

Figure 49. Foramen Magnum Angle and Walking Angle Comparison (Chimps to Humans).[202]

One study conducted by evolutionary scientists showed that the angle of the foraman magnum of Lucy's species was "well below the range for our sample of modern humans but

138

overlaps the low end of the range for position between modern apes and humans, but closer to the former (chimpanzees, specifically)."[203]

Fatal Flaw #2: Lucy's Semicircular Canals

Humans have three semicircular canals embedded deep within our ears that are integrated with our brains, heads, and eyes to keep us balanced as we move. Apes' semicircular canals orient to their up-tilted heads. To investigate how these semicircular canals are involved in the movement of various creatures, scientists have studied them in depth using advanced scanning techniques and making measurements of their different structures. *Australopithecines*, as well as other living and non-living apes, all have semicircular canals that fit ape-oriented heads that fit bodies designed for walking on all fours, whereas humans semicircular canals match upright, two legged locomotion.

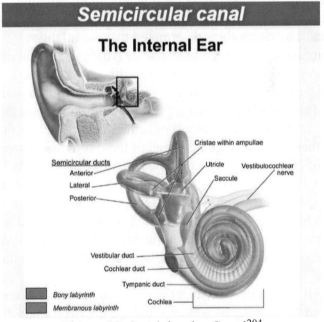

Figure 50. Semicircular Canal[204]

In particular, they learned that the semicircular canals of *Australopithecines* were best suited for "facultative bipedalism,"[205] which means walking occasionally on two feet, just like many apes walk today. While this study focused on *Australopithecus africanus*—and Lucy's species has been labeled *Australopithecus afarensis*—they are anatomically similar.[206]

What about Lucy's species specifically? Dr. Bernard Wood conducted a study that revealed that the semicircular canals of Lucy's species "were more like those of chimpanzees than of modern humans. The fluid-filled semicircular canals are crucial in maintaining balance, and so all three lines of evidence suggest that the locomotion of *Australopithecus afarensis* was *unlikely to have been restricted to walking on two feet*"[207] (emphasis added).

Another report in the leading secular science journal *Scientific American*[208] reviewed the research conducted on a baby *Australopithecus afarensis*, stating: "Using computed tomographic imaging, the team was able to glimpse her semicircular canal system, which is important for maintaining balance. The researchers determined that the infant's semicircular canals resemble those of African apes and other *Australopithecines* (such as *Australopithecus africanus*). This, they suggest, could indicate the *Australopithecus afarensis* was not as fast and agile on two legs as we modern humans are."

One fascinating aspect of semicircular canals is that, while they all work together, each of them provides a separate sense of directional balance: "The superior canal detects head rotations on the anterior-posterior (side-to-side movement, like tilting the head toward the shoulders) axis. The posterior canal detects rotations on the sagittal plane (forward and backward movement, like sit-ups). The horizontal canal senses movement on a vertical basis, as the head rotates up-and-down on the neck."[209]

It just so happens that the two same canals that are most involved for helping us walk upright are the two canals that are *statistically significantly different*[210] between humans and

140

chimps. Lucy's species clearly identifies with chimps. Dr. Spoor noted that two of the three semicircular canals in particular coordinate "upright bipedal behavior" because they are involved in "movements in the vertical plane" (i.e., upright walking). [211] Drs. Day and Fitzpatrick agree with this, stating: "The anterior and posterior canals of the human vestibular organs are enlarged in size relative to the horizontal canal whereas the three canals are more equal in size in other species. The significance of this is that the anterior and posterior canals are orientated to sense rotation in the vertical planes, *the movements that are important for controlling upright balance*"[212] (emphasis added).

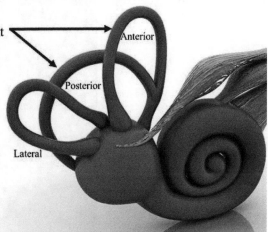

These two are most associated with upright walking, and they are significantly different between apes/Lucy's species and humans.

Anterior

Posterior

Lateral

Figure 51. Semicircular Canals[213]

What difference does this make? Well, think about it this way: If you had your semicircular canals surgically replaced with a chimp's, at the very least, you'd be really disoriented! Your head would feel level only when you were looking to the sky. You wouldn't be able to run with as much ease as you have now, since the same two semicircular canals that are significantly different between apes and humans help stabilize your head when running.[214]

Fatal Flaw #3: Lucy's Mystery Vertebra

In 2015, press releases started coming out and showing that, even after 40 years of study involving hundreds of scientists, one of Lucy's bones (a vertebra) didn't even belong to her![215] In fact, it didn't even belong to Lucy's species, but was from a *Theropithecus*, a type of baboon. Does that make you wonder if we're really dealing with bones from a single individual with Lucy? Especially when Lucy was put together from hundreds of bone fragments that were found scattered along a hillside?[216]

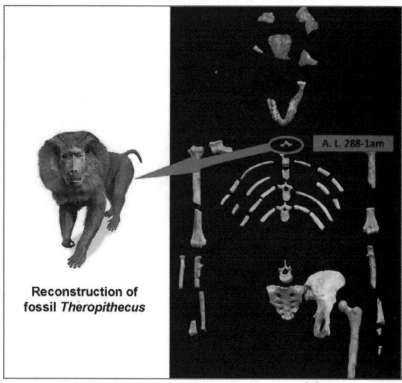

Figure 52. Lucy's "Extra" Vertebra.[217]

Fatal Flaw #4: Lucy's Pelvis

Next, we have Lucy's pelvis, which Johanson's team believed was "broken apart and then fused together during later fossilization…" which caused it to "be in an anatomically impossible position" and to "flare out like a chimp's pelvis."[218]

Their solution to this problem was to use a power saw to cut it apart and then piece it back together! After "fixing" the pelvis, they noted: "It was a tricky job, but after taking the kink out of the pelvis, it all fit together perfectly, like a three-dimensional jigsaw puzzle. As a result, the angle of the hip looks nothing like a chimp's, but a lot like ours…"[219]

Even secular scientists who hold to evolution have problems with Lucy's pelvis reconstruction, stating "We think that the reconstruction overestimates the width of this [pelvis] area, creating a very human-like sacral plane,"[220] and another stated, "The fact that the anterior portion of the iliac blade faces

laterally in humans but not in chimpanzees is obvious. The marked resemblance of AL 288-1 [Lucy] to the chimpanzee is equally obvious."[221] Charles Oxnard, evolutionist and author of the *Order of Man*, stated that her bones seemed to show that she was a "real swinger… based on anatomical data, *Australopithecines* must have been arboreal [tree-dwelling] … Lucy's pelvis shows a flare that is better suited for climbing than for walking."[222] Isn't it interesting how these remarks from evolutionary scientists never make their way into public school textbooks? Instead, Lucy is typically shown walking upright, as shown in Figure 53.

Figure 53. Lucy in Public School Textbooks.[223]

143

Fatal Flaw #5: Lucy's Locking Wrists

Lucy had locking wrists like quadruped apes, not like humans.[224] This has been widely reported in both scientific journals as well as the general media. For example, even the *San Diego Union Tribune* reported, "A chance discovery made by looking at a cast of the bones of 'Lucy,' the most famous fossil of *Australopithecus afarensis*, shows her wrist was stiff, like a chimpanzee's, Brian Richmond and David Strait of George Washington University in Washington, D.C., reported. This suggests that her ancestors walked on their knuckles."[225] The study conducted by these scientists concluded: "Measurements of the shape of wristbones (distal radius) showed that Lucy's type were knuckle walkers, similar to gorillas."[226]

When interviewed about their study (published in *Nature*) they stated: "It suddenly occurred to me that paleoanthropologists had never looked at the wrists of Lucy or other important early human ancestors discovered since the early papers were published...." so while they were visiting the Smithsonian, they went to the cast collection, inspected Lucy's radius [forearm bone], and found that she had the "classic knuckle-walking feature." This became obvious when they "saw a ridge of bone on the lower forearm that prevented Lucy's wrist, like that of a chimpanzee or gorilla, from rocking backward, but allowed it to lock in an upright position for easy knuckle-walking."[227] Figure 54 highlights this "locking wrist" feature they found on Lucy's bones.

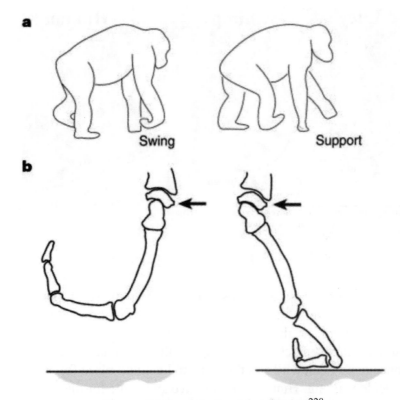

Figure 54. Lucy's Locking Wrist.[228]

The study conducted by Richmond and Strait revealed that Lucy had the same concave arm bone that joined with her convex wrist, creating a locking system that allowed for both swinging and stable knuckle-walking (as shown in Figure 55).

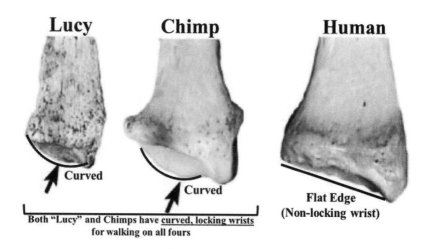

Figure 55. Lucy's Locking Wrist.[229]

Figure 55 shows a close-up view from the study. The arm bone on the far left is from Lucy; the one in the middle is from a chimp; and the one on the far right is human. Notice how Lucy's bone is matches the chimp's—they both have the concave shape that allows the wrist to lock into place for knuckle walking. Humans do not have any angle for this whatsoever because we're not designed for walking on our hands!

Fatal Flaw #6: Lucy's Curved Fingers

Next, we'll take a look at the fingers of Lucy's species. Comparison of various apes, humans, and Lucy's species' finger curvatures reveal some major differences. Even evolutionary scientists have admitted that the curved fingers of Lucy's species were best suited for swinging in trees.[230] One study statistically compared various finger measurements from several different types of apes against humans, and grouped the fingers of Lucy's species in the same category as chimps and bonobos, and far away from human's straight fingers (see Figures 56 and 57).

146

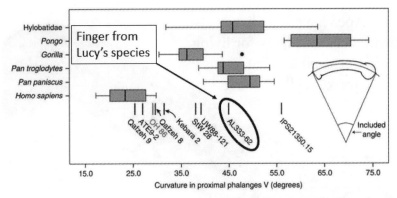

Figure 56. Finger Curvature Study Revealing Lucy's Species Is Categorized with Apes and Gorillas.[231]

Figure 57 shows a finger from one of Lucy's species, showing significant curvature compared to human fingers, which are not curved.

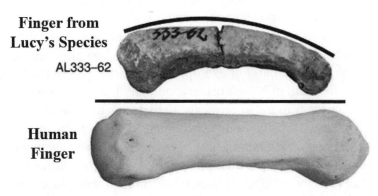

Figure 57. Finger from Lucy's Species Compared to Human Finger.[232]

Other examples of *Australopithecine* apes had curved fingers and ape-like limb proportions that point toward her kind as living in trees, so the same was probably true of Lucy.[233]

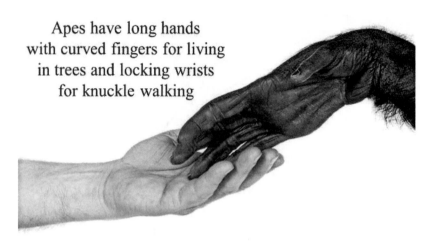

Apes have long hands with curved fingers for living in trees and locking wrists for knuckle walking

Figure 58. Human and Chimp Hands.

Fatal Flaw #7: Lucy's Short Little Legs

Some evolutionary scientists have argued that Lucy's legs were much too short for upright walking. Some say she walked with a "bent-hip, bent-knee" method; some say she might have "shuffled"; some say she walked on all fours; some say she was bipedal. For example, Dr. Bill Jungers at the Stony Brook Institute in New York argued that "Lucy's legs were too short, in relation to her arms, for her species to have achieved a fully modern adaptation to bipedalism."[234] Drs. Stern and Sussman advocated that Lucy's species would have walked "bent-hip, bent-knee" method, much like a living chimpanzee, because of the number of skeletal features in their skeletons which are functionally associated with arboreality in living apes (e.g., curved phalanges, long trunk but short legs, etc.).[235] Dr. Hunt argued that the most efficient behavior for Lucy's species would have been "bipedal posture augmented with bipedal shuffling" as a consequence of anatomical compromise between the needs of terrestrial bipedality and arboreal climbing.[236]

Without any of Lucy's species alive today, one cannot know for certain how they moved around. But that hasn't stopped several scientists—from both the evolution and creation

148

camps—from speculating about it. As we have reviewed in this section, however, plenty of evidence *from evolutionary scientists* indicates she likely walked on all fours (including her semicircular canals, skull, locking wrists, curved fingers, and now, her short legs).

Fatal Flaw #8: The Widespread Exaggeration of Lucy's Human-like Appearance

Lucy was originally found in *hundreds* of pieces before she was painstakingly glued together in the way they believed she was before she died. Even though many of the first reports that came out after Lucy was discovered stated that Lucy's skeleton was "40% complete,"[237] Lucy's discoverer (Johanson) clarified this in a book published 22 years after Lucy was found, stating: "Lucy's skeleton consists of some 47 out of 207 bones, including parts of upper and lower limbs, the backbone, ribs and the pelvis. With the exception of the mandible [lower jaw] the skull is represented only by five vault fragments, and most of the hand and foot bones are missing."[238] This computes to actually **23%** of the complete skeleton (47 ÷ 206), not "about 40%."

Numerous artists have drawn Lucy with human feet even though the fossil lacked both hand and foot bones. Frustratingly for those who care about truth, these illustrations continue to ignore subsequent finds, revealing that *Australopithecines* had curved ape fingers and grasping ape feet. Figure 59 shows how Lucy is represented at public exhibits, such as those found at the St. Louis Zoo and Denver Museum of Nature and Science.

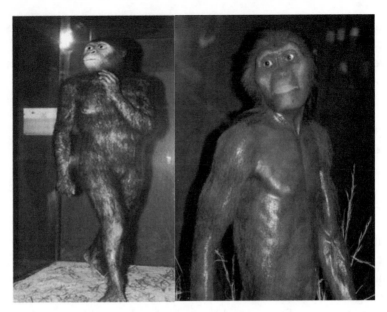

Figure 59. Lucy at Public Exhibits (Zoos and Museums). Lucy at the St. Louis Zoo (Left) and at the Denver Museum of Nature and Science (Right).[239]

Most Lucy models show her with white sclera of the eye visible, even though 100% of all apes alive today have eyes that look dark because the sclera is not visible. Do you think this was done to make her look more human-like?

It's amazing how they can find hundreds of bone fragments scattered across a hillside in a nine-foot radius[240] that supposedly lay in the soil for over 3 million years and reconstruct a human-like Lucy, complete with eyewhites displayed in museums around the world! At least one bone belonging to a completely different animal was mistaken for Lucy's for over 40 years. Were there others?

Figure 60. Making Lucy Look Human from Hundreds of Bones Fragments, Glue, and Imagination.

To further exaggerate Lucy's human-like appearance, some Lucy models don't even have hair! (see Figure 61).

Figure 61. Hairless Lucy Walking with her "Family," including Incorrect (Human) Feet and Hands. [241]

Fatal Flaw #9: Gender

A great deal of debate has emerged even over Lucy's gender, with some scientists arguing that the evidence shows she was actually a male! Articles with catchy titles have emerged such as "Lucy or Lucifer? [242] and more recently, "Lucy or Brucey?"[243] If evolutionists are so certain that we evolved from Lucy-like creatures, but they can't seem to even determine the gender of the leading human evolution icon, what other assumptions are being made?

Fatal Flaw #10: Falling out of a Tree to Her Death

Now we move onto the most recent news about Lucy. In 2016 the University of Texas had a team of orthopedic surgeons reveal the findings of a study that evaluated the numerous "compression" and "greenstick" fractures in Lucy's skeleton. A greenstick fracture goes by this name because it's the type of bone break that occurs under compression or fast bending—much like a green stick would break when such force is applied.

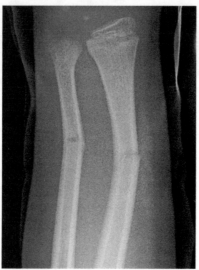

Figure 62. Greenstick Fracture[244]

This team determined that Lucy most likely died while falling 40 feet out of a tree traveling 35 miles per hour, and was "conscious when she reached the ground" because of the way she tried to break her fall. Even the lead study scientist, John Kappelman, remarks, "It is ironic that the fossil at the center of a debate about the role of arborealism (living in trees) in human evolution likely died from injuries suffered from a fall out of a tree."[245] Yes, it is quite ironic that Lucy, the supposed human ancestor who walked on two feet, died while falling 40 feet out of a tree.

But they've even offered a "rescuing device," stating that "because Lucy was both terrestrial and arboreal, features that permitted her to move efficiently on the ground may have compromised her ability to climb trees, predisposing her species to more frequent falls." So, to save the embarrassment of the "bipedal ape" dying by falling out of a tree, they believe that she must have fallen out of a tree because she wasn't used to living in them anymore." That's quite a reach for a creature that supposedly lived over 3 million years ago!

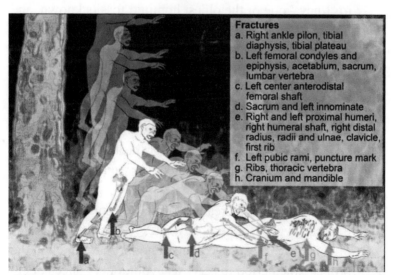

Fractures
a. Right ankle pilon, tibial diaphysis, tibial plateau
b. Left femoral condyles and epiphysis, acetabulum, sacrum, lumbar vertebra
c. Left center anterodistal femoral shaft
d. Sacrum and left innominate
e. Right and left proximal humeri, right humeral shaft, right distal radius, radii and ulnae, clavicle, first rib
f. Left pubic rami, puncture mark
g. Ribs, thoracic vertebra
h. Cranium and mandible

Figure 63. Lucy, the Supposedly Bipedal Ape, Falling 40-Feet from a Tree to Her Death.[246]

153

In summary, consider these conclusions about Lucy that were drawn from leading evolutionary scientists:

- Dr. Charles Oxnard (professor of anatomy) wrote, "The *Australopithecines* known over the last several decades … are now irrevocably removed from a place in the evolution of human bipedalism … All this should make us wonder about the usual presentation of human evolution in introductory textbooks."[247]
- Dr. Solly Zuckerman heads the Department of Anatomy of the University of Birmingham in England and is a scientific adviser to the highest level of the British government. He studied Australopithecus fossils for 15 years with a team of scientists and concluded, "They are just apes."[248]
- Dr. Wray Herbert admits that his fellow paleoanthropologists "compare the pygmy chimpanzee to 'Lucy,' one of the oldest hominid fossils known, and finds the similarities striking. They are almost identical in body size, in stature and in brain size."[249]
- Dr. Albert W. Mehlert said, "the evidence… makes it overwhelmingly likely that Lucy was no more than a variety of pygmy chimpanzee, and walked the same way (awkwardly upright on occasions, but mostly quadrupedal). The 'evidence' for the alleged transformation from ape to man is extremely unconvincing."[250]
- Marvin Lubenow, Creation researcher and author of the book *Bones of Contention,* wrote, "There are no fossils of Australopithecus or of any other primate stock in the proper time period to serve as evolutionary ancestors to humans. *As far as we can tell from the fossil record,*

when humans first appear in the fossil record they are already human"[251] (emphasis added).

- Drs. DeWitt Steele and Gregory Parker concluded: "Australopithecus can probably be dismissed [from human evolution] as a type of extinct chimpanzee."[252]

In reality, the remains of these ape-like creatures occur in small-scale deposits that rest on top of broadly extending flood deposits. They were probably fossilized after Noah's Flood, during the Ice Age, when tremendous rains and residual volcanic explosions buried Ice Age creatures.[253] Answers in Genesis provides a rendition of what Lucy most likely looked like (Figure 64).

Figure 64. What Lucy Most Likely Looked Like (Credit: Answers in Genesis Presentation Library).

Chapter 6: Evolution vs. God
What's Wrong with the Idea That God Used Evolution to Create Everything (Theistic Evolution)?

In a nutshell, theistic evolution is the belief that God used biological evolution as the process to bring about the variety of life on Earth over millions of years. The Bible plainly disagrees with theistic evolution. In fact, they are opposites, as will be shown below.

More and more student-aged Christians are becoming theistic evolutionists—especially those who are raised in public school and don't receive much biblical training at home or in church.

One of the most common testimonies we hear from high schoolers goes something like this: They become Christians at a young age, but they don't get much training in doctrine, especially creation-evolution related topics. After being saturated in public school evolutionary teaching (and not hearing the Biblical Creation view from parents or church leaders), they start developing *cognitive dissonance*—the tension that develops when holding two contradictory beliefs. They begin questioning: "I know that God exists, but they seem to present so much credible evidence for evolution at school, and it seems like the 'smart scientists' tend to believe it." Many take the shortest route to resolving this mental tension by adopting a worldview that is somewhere between their Christian faith and evolution. Without even knowing it, they have just adopted the view of theistic evolution.

In one subtle play, the enemy has replaced their belief in an all-powerful God who spoke creation into existence over six days and His inerrant Word with a "god" who creates life through a process of death and suffering. If true, the Bible wouldn't really mean what it says! While some might believe there's nothing wrong with this belief, we'll challenge that perspective next by reviewing the six fatal flaws with theistic evolution.

The Six Fatal Flaws of Theistic Evolution

We've distilled the major problems of theistic evolution into a list of the top six. As we'll see, the problems with theistic evolution are not just some abstract theological problems—they bring a serious impact in the daily lives of believers. After all, our beliefs form the roots of our actions and the sum of our actions make up our lives and our choices.

Adam Versus Apes: Theistic Evolution Denies the Biblical Creation of Adam and Makes Apes Our Ancestors

The Bible is clear that Adam was made spontaneously and supernaturally by God, in God's own image and likeness, out of the dust of the Earth (Genesis 1:26 and following). We are not made in the image of some lower ape-like creature, and the "image" of God and His "likeness" does not match that of an ape.

Making this idea even worse, evolution would have humans shaped as we are today only because our particular line of ape-like ancestors out-lasted and even out-killed other varieties. This is a far cry from humans being specially created out of the dust of the Earth in the image of a loving and intentional God. Jesus Himself clearly disagreed with the ideas that millions of years of human evolution occurred by stating, "But from the *beginning* of the creation, God 'made them male and female'" (Mark 10:6) (emphasis added).

Biblical Order of Creation

The basic order of the Creation account in Genesis 1 disagrees with the modern theory of how evolution supposedly unfolded from the formation of the universe to life on Earth (see Table 9).

157

Table 9. Differences between the Bible and Evolution.

Bible	Evolution
Earth before the sun	Sun before the earth
Oceans before land	Land before oceans
Land plants first	Oceanlife first
Fish before insects	Insects before fish
Plants before sun	Sun before plants
Birds before reptiles	Reptiles before birds
God created man instantly after all other animals were created	The process of death created man, and evolution is still occuring, though invisible because it takes millions of years

Table 9 clearly lays out how the Biblical order of Creation is opposite to how evolution supposedly happened.

Theistic Evolution Makes Death, and not God, Our Creator

No matter which "version" of evolution one holds to—whether naturalistic evolution without a God, or theistic evolution with a process started by God and left to run its course, or progressive creation where God uses cosmological and geological evolution while occasionally wiping out and creating new life forms along the way—the core problem is that the process of *death is setup as the creator of life.*

Each of these versions of evolution has a bloody, competitive, "survival of the fittest" process as the creator of new life forms. Each starts from lower life forms and eventually leads to man over millions of years. There are some serious problems with this view, and it could not differ more from the biblical account! What kind of all-powerful God would need to use a cruel, experimental process to bring about the variety of life on earth?

The idea of *punctuated equilibrium* (a view even held, in some form, by many progressive creationists) holds that God advances evolutionary development by isolated episodes of rapid speciation between long periods of little or no change. In

158

other words, God used "random, wasteful, inefficiencies" to create the world into which Adam was placed.[254] God didn't get it right the first time, so He had to experiment through a cruel random process as a means to advance new life forms?

To the contrary, the Bible holds that God initially created everything perfect, and then our sin initiated the process of death, suffering, and bloodshed. How could God look upon all His Creation and call it "very good" (Genesis 1:31) if animals (and later humans) were tearing each other apart to survive...for millions of years before Adam? Why would an all-powerful, loving, merciful God need to use a blood-filled, clumsy, random process to populate the Earth with animal variety? God's initial Creation was perfect, but we messed it up!

Yes, we see natural selection and survival of the fittest going on in today's world, but this process is a "mindless" one without creative agency. For example, consider a large field with a healthy population of grasshoppers in two color varieties, green and yellow. When the fields are green in the springtime, the green grasshoppers may thrive more than the yellow ones because they blend in to their surroundings, being less visible to their predators. Then, in the fall when the fields turn yellow, this process is reversed, and the yellow grasshoppers thrive. Is this natural selection producing new species? Certainly not! Rather, the pre-programmed gene variability that God installed into the grasshoppers interacts with their environment. The grasshoppers are all still grasshoppers! We see the same principle in oscillating bird beak shapes in Darwin's finches which are proudly used to promote evolution in today's school textbooks.

Theistic Evolution Places Death before Sin

Perhaps the most serious problem with theistic evolution is that it has man coming on the scene after billions of years of death-filled evolution has taken place. This makes the brutal "survival of the fittest" process God's idea instead of the consequence of sin. To the contrary, according to the Bible, when man appears in Creation, he is perfect and sinless and there's no such thing as death. Death does not come into the picture *until man sins* ("but of the tree of the knowledge of good and evil you shall not eat, for in the day that you eat of it you shall surely die," Genesis 2:17). So, you can't have death of mankind before the Fall of man and have a logical foundation for the Gospel (see also Romans 5:12 and 1 Corinthians 15:22).

In addition to God clearly warning Adam that "death will come" if he sins, two stark truths in Genesis address this important "death before sin" topic.

First, animals did not eat each other at the beginning of Creation, and thus there was no "survival of the fittest" or "natural selection" process that could supposedly work to drive evolution forward. Humans and animals originally ate vegetation:

> And God said, 'See, I have given you every herb that yields seed which is on the face of all the earth, and every tree whose fruit yields seed; to you it shall be for food. Also, to every beast of the earth, to every bird of the air, and to everything that creeps on the earth, in which there is life, I have given every green herb for food' (Genesis 1:29–30).

God did not endorse humans using animals as a food source until *after* the Flood: "Everything that lives and moves about will be food for you. *Just as I gave you the green plants, I now give you everything*" (Genesis 9:3, emphasis added). Further, it seems that God put the fear of man into animals *after* the Flood because they would be a food source from that point forward: "And the fear of you and the dread of you shall be on every beast of the earth, on every bird of the air, on all that move on the earth, and on all the fish of the sea" (Genesis 9:2).

Second, how could God look over the billions of years of blood-filled "survival of the fittest" evolution until it finally reached man and then call Creation "very good" (Genesis

160

1:31)? This would make Adam's sin and the curse of death meaningless, because death had already existed for millennia! If death was used to create Adam and Eve, what was the real consequence of sin?

Figure 65. Is this a "very good" creation? Carnivorism entered the world after sin.

God's original creation was perfect. The first chapter of Genesis states six times that what God had made was "good" and the seventh time that "God saw everything that He had made, and indeed it was *very* good" (Genesis 1:31). Now, however, we can look at the world around us and see there has been an obvious change. Many animals live by predation. Lions eat their prey while still alive. Bears eat young deer shortly after they are born.

If God created a perfect world at the beginning and animals were first designed as vegetarians, how did these defense and attack structures (like fangs and claws) come about? There are two primary perspectives on this topic, so we'll briefly review each.

The first is that these features were not originally used for carnivorism. In other words, the design was the same but the function was different. Take sharp teeth, for example. Panda bears have incredibly sharp teeth, but 99% of their diet is bamboo.[255] The same is true for numerous other creatures that appear to be vicious meat-eaters, but have a primarily vegetarian diet.

Figure 66. Pandas eat bamboo, but have teeth structures that appear to be designed as a "meat-eater."

Vicious-looking canine teeth aren't just used for carnivorism, they are also used in communication. For example, many apes, dogs, cats, and other animals expose their canines to express dominance, ownership of mates, and guard territory. The same teeth that are used by wolves for killing and eating are used by dogs today for eating domestic dog food. Even sharp claws that are used today for predation are used in many cases for climbing and defense. So, this first view avoids suggesting that God's initial design features were intended to be harmful to other creatures in His creation.

One of the limitations with this first viewpoint is that it excludes animals from changes that the Fall certainly introduced to the other parts of Creation, such as thorns and thistles being introduced to plants. Genesis 3:17–19 is clear that plants were cursed by man's Fall with thorns and thistles, and plants use thorns primarily as a defense mechanism. Were animals exempt from similar changes that were introduced by the Fall?

The second viewpoint is that defense and attack features were introduced by God as a result of the Fall. However, it is not a widely-held Biblical Creation position that animals quickly and recently developed all physical features used for predation. This is because physical change was not required to make plant-eaters into meat-eaters; it was merely a change in *behavior*, as many of the features that are useful today for predation are also useful for eating plants. It is also interesting to note that many predators have to learn to kill, as many "social predators" (e.g., lions) are not born with the knowledge of how to hunt and kill—they are behaviors that are learned from the other animals in their group.

Let's apply these two viewpoints on one of the most "obviously carnivorous" animals of all time—*Smilodon*, the saber-toothed cat. Named after its scissor-like front teeth (some over six inches in length), this massive lion looks like a perfect killing machine. In fact, the two massive teeth even lack lateral (side to side) motion that would be necessary if it were a vegetarian. Biblical Creationist and Biologist, Dr. Nathaniel Jeanson addresses this challenge by stating:

> How did these big cats acquire their sharp teeth? At the Curse, God probably didn't speak sharp teeth into existence out of nothing. His acts of global creation were finished by day seven of the creation week (Genesis 2:1–3; Exodus 20:11; Hebrews 4:3). So where did the lion's teeth come from? … God may have created creatures with latent genetic information to be "switched on" only after Genesis 3, a concept similar to the "mediated design" model. Alternatively, God may have created anatomical and physiological features capable of multiple purposes. Powerful jaws, now used to kill and tear flesh, may have

initially been used to open fruits and plant seeds of the size and hardness of modern watermelons and coconuts. Could the lion's teeth have been used for tearing tough plants and roots in the beginning? Biblically, this latter hypothesis is compelling. Consider the effects of the reversal of the Curse in Isaiah 11:6–7: 'The wolf also shall dwell with the lamb, and the leopard shall lie down with the kid; and the calf and the young lion and the fatling together...*the lion shall eat straw like the ox.*' In reversing the Curse, God doesn't seem to change the lion's anatomy; He simply changes the lion's behavior. Furthermore, Scripture explicitly mentions God switching the mental states of animals after the Flood (Genesis 9:2). Might He also have done something much like this at the Curse?[256] (emphasis added)

The Believer Loses the Power That Comes from Fully Believing in God's Word

Put simply, there is power that comes from fully believing in the Word of God. A straight-forward reading of the Bible's account of origins as laid out in Genesis 1 and 5 and Exodus 20:11—without spin or interpreting it through man's lens of "science"—will lead an honest reader to six days of Creation just thousands of years ago. If God really used evolution to create everything, He could have simply told Moses to write it down that way! But He didn't, and the Creation account reads much differently than how it might read if evolution took place over millions of years. The Bible is clear in several places that God "spoke" creation into existence.

Compromising on God's Word by agreeing with theistic evolution robs the Christian of the power that comes from standing fully on the Word of God, and claiming its authority. When Dr. Charles Jackson with Creation Truth Foundation was

164

asked, "Do you meet many Christians at college who are drifting away from the faith?" his response was eye-opening:

> They're more than being drifted away from the faith; there's a current that's created under them that pulls them away from the faith. When you put a question mark after any Bible verses that don't have them there already (or verses that give a disclaimer like, 'this is a mystery'), like 'in six days the Lord God created heaven and earth and all that's in them' (Exodus 20:11), instantly you have a quantum drop in the joy and power of the Christian walk—all of the gifts of God in you—you can feel it. It's like someone pulled the plug and you are running on battery now, and a low battery at that. [257]

There is a close association between the Word of God and the Power of God (Hebrews 4:12, 6:5; Matthew 22:29). Can a Christian live a power-filled life and walk in God's will while denying the Word of God? Christians will live a more power-filled life when they strongly align what they believe and how they live to the Word of God. Every stanza of Psalm 119 mentions the Word in some way for this reason.

Denying God's special creation and not believing that He created the world by His Word (Hebrews 11:3; Psalm 33:6) creates a deep crack in the foundation of a Christian, even in ways that are sometimes not known by the person doubting. John Macarthur[258] adds to this discussing by stating:

> Christians will get out there, saying "Boy, we're against abortion, and we're against homosexuality, and we're against Jack Kevorkian because he's murdering people, and we're against euthanasia, and we're against genocide and, you know, we're against the moral evils of our society, etc." Why are we against

those things? Can you tell me why? Why are we against those things? Give me one reason. Here it is, because they're forbidden in Scripture. Is that not true? The only reason we're against abortion is because God's against it. How do we know that? Because it's in the Word of God. The reason we're against homosexuality, adultery, etc. is because of the Bible. You see, we stand on the Scripture. But the problem is we don't want to stand on the Scripture in Genesis. So we equivocate on whether or not the Bible is an authority at all. What do you think the watching world thinks about our commitment to Scripture? Pretty selective, isn't it?

Theistic Evolution Has Christ Dying for the Sins of a Mythical Adam

The genealogies in Genesis 5 and 10 and Luke 3 lead directly back to Adam, the first man created by God. But if these genealogies don't lead back to a real Adam who actually sinned, then who do they lead back to? Because the "sinner" Adam and the Savior Jesus are linked together in Romans 5:16–18, any theological view which mythologizes Adam undermines the biblical basis of Jesus' work of redemption.

Conclusion

Is Genesis history? Do scientific discoveries nullify the Word of God? Our six chapters offer clear answers. First, an immense weight of historical evidence proves beyond reasonable doubt that the Bible really does contain the same exact message that God originally inspired within the prophets and apostles who first penned His Words. In particular, the Dead Sea Scrolls proved that 2,000 years' worth of copying accumulated only minor changes like alternate spellings, and changed not one basic doctrine. Second, since the Bible really is God's Word, we should pay close attention to whatever it says. And it clearly teaches a recent creation. All attempts to squeeze millions of years into the text devalue God's Word.

Bible believers should find encouragement in how thoroughly science confirms the fact of creation, the Flood, and even the timing of Biblical Creation. We learned that radioisotope dating techniques rely on unproven assumptions like how much of each isotope inhabited the rock back when it cooled. Wrong radioisotope "ages" for rocks of known age, plus conflicting radioisotope "ages" for the same rock demonstrate that radioisotope dating does not work. Those "ages" are only as good as the assumptions they make, and they clearly make bad assumptions. Next, if Noah's Flood really happened, then one should expect exactly what dinosaur and other fossils show: widespread catastrophic watery burial and proteins that last thousands but not a million years. Finally, we learned that even evolutionists debate every "transitional" pre-human candidate, and every "transitional" feature. In other words, for every evolutionary researcher who promotes one human ancestral feature, another one contests it. "Human evolution" is fraught with fraud and storytelling about fossils that merely signify extinct ape and human varieties.

The last chapter highlighted flaws with the idea that God used evolution. No, He didn't. If He did, then his declaration in Genesis 1:31, "Then God saw everything that He had made, and indeed it was very good" was not very good. But fortunately for those willing to take God at His word, good science confirms exactly what He said in Genesis and throughout the Bible about creation and the Flood.

Does any of this even matter? Are we splitting theological hairs that have no significance in daily life? Let's allow the Bible to answer this question. Romans is arguably the cornerstone of Paul's writings in the New Testament. This key book begins by describing a process of depravity—which can apply to both individuals and nations—that starts with denying God as the Creator and His Word:

> For the wrath of God is revealed from heaven against all ungodliness and unrighteousness of men, who suppress the truth in unrighteousness, because what may be known of God is manifest in them, for God has shown it to them. For since the creation of the world His invisible attributes are clearly seen, being understood by the things that are made, even His eternal power and Godhead, so that they are without excuse, because, although they knew God, they did not glorify Him as God, nor were thankful, but became futile in their thoughts, and their foolish hearts were darkened. Professing to be wise, they became fools...

This passage continues by describing what happens to individuals and nations that continue down this path, which includes a host of consequences we are watching unfold before our eyes in America. Those who deny God as the Creator will be "given over" to the consequences of their disbelief and their willing denial of His truth—a truth that they ultimately know exists, but choose to deny: "And just as they did not see fit to acknowledge God any longer, God gave them over to a depraved mind, to do those things which are not proper..." (Romans 1:28, NASB).

168

My daughter had the opportunity to watch this passage in action while attending her college Anthropology class. The professor was showing a video that demonstrated the complex nature of DNA and the incredible "auto-replicating" DNA process. A student asked, "How does it *know* how to do that? How do the different parts of the DNA building process *know* how to work together?" Stunned, the professor explained, "It just does—perhaps a geneticist can explain it better." The student retreated, knowing deep down that the professor's answer was not enough.

Research has shown that **44%** of young adults who abandon their Christian faith started developing their doubts in high school.[259] When these "ex-Christians" were asked, "What makes you question the Bible the most," **40%** gave responses that had to do with Biblical Creation, including Noah's Flood, the age of the earth, and the Genesis account. Students need to be equipped on Creation Apologetics before (and during) attending public school classes that starkly contrast the Biblical Creation account.

This book has been one step along that journey. To equip students for the specific evolution-based arguments they are presented in public school, we recommend our six-lesson, video based "Debunk Evolution" program, which can be downloaded free (*www.debunkevolution.com*) or purchased in hard copy from our website (*www.genesisapologetics.com*).

Praise the Lord from the heavens; praise Him in the heights! Praise Him, all His angels; praise Him, all His hosts! Praise Him, sun and moon; praise Him, all you stars of light! Praise Him, you heavens of heavens, and you waters above the heavens! Let them praise the name of the Lord, *for He commanded and they were created*.
—Psalms 148:1–5

Helpful Resources

The following websites are recommended for further research:

- Genesis Apologetics: *www.genesisapologetics.com*
- Debunking Evolution: *www.debunkevolution.com*
  Answers in Genesis: *www.answersingenesis.org*
- Answers in Genesis (High School Biology): *www.evolutionexposed.com*
- Creation Ministries International: *www.cmi.org*
- Creation Today: *www.creationtoday.org*
- Creation Wiki*: www.creationwiki.org*
- Evolution: The Grand Experiment with by Dr. Carl Werner: *www.thegrandexperiment.com*
- The Institute for Creation Research: *www.ICR.org*

Prayer of Salvation

You're not here by accident—God *loves* you and He *knows* who you are like no one else. His Word says:

> Lord, You have searched me and known me.
> You know my sitting down and my rising up;
> you understand my thought afar off. You
> comprehend my path and my lying down, and
> are acquainted with all my ways. For there is not
> a word on my tongue, but behold, O Lord, You
> know it altogether. You have hedged me behind
> and before, and laid Your hand upon me. Such
> knowledge is too wonderful for me; It is high, I
> cannot attain it. (Psalm 139:1–6)

God loves you with an everlasting love, and with a love that can cover all of your transgressions—all that you have ever done wrong. But you have to repent of those sins and trust the Lord Jesus Christ for forgiveness. Your past is in the past. He wants to give you a new future and new hope.

But starting this new journey requires a step—a step of faith. God has already reached out to you as far as He can. By giving His son to die for your sins on the Cross, He's done everything He can to reach out to you. The next step is yours to take, and this step requires faith to receive His son into your heart. It also requires repentance (turning away) from your past sins–a surrendered heart that is willing to reject a sinful lifestyle. Many believers have a much easier time leaving sinful lifestyles after they fully trust Jesus and nobody else and nothing else. Along with forgiveness, the Holy Spirit enters your life when you receive Jesus, and He will lead you into a different lifestyle and way—a way that will lead to blessing, joy, patient endurance under trials, and eternal life.

If you are ready to receive Him, then you would recognize these key Biblical truths.[260]

1. Acknowledge that your sin separates you from God. The Bible describes sin in many ways. Most simply, sin is our failure to measure up to God's holiness and His righteous standards. We sin by things we do, choices we make, attitudes we show, and thoughts we entertain. We also sin when we fail to do right things or even think right thoughts. The Bible also says that all people are sinners: "there is none righteous, not even one." No matter how good we try to be, none of us does right things all the time. The Bible is clear, "For all have sinned and come short of the glory of God" (Romans 3:23).

2. Our sins demand punishment—the punishment of death and separation from God. However, because of His great love, God sent His only Son Jesus to die for our sins: "God demonstrates His own love for us in this: While we were still sinners, Christ died for us" (Romans 5:8). For you to come to God you have to get rid of your sin problem. But, in our own strength, not one of us can do this! You can't make yourself right with God by being a better person. Only God can rescue us from our sins. He is willing to do this not because of anything you can offer Him, but **just because He loves you**! "He saved us, not because of righteous things we had done, but because of His mercy" (Titus 3:5).

3. It's only God's grace that allows you to come to Him— not your efforts to "clean up your life" or work your way to Heaven. You can't earn it. It's a free gift: "For it is by grace you have been saved, through faith—and this not from yourselves, it is the gift of God—not by works, so that no one can boast" (Ephesians 2:8–9).

4. For you to come to God, the penalty for your sin must be paid. God's gift to you is His son, Jesus, who paid the debt for you when He died on the Cross. "For the wages of sin is death, but the gift of God is eternal life in Jesus Christ our Lord" (Romans 6:23). God brought Jesus

back from the dead. He provided the way for you to have a personal relationship with Him through Jesus.

When we realize how deeply our sin grieves the heart of God and how desperately we need a Savior, we are ready to receive God's offer of salvation. To admit we are sinners means turning away from our sin and selfishness and turning to follow Jesus. The Bible word for this is "repentance"—to change our thinking to acknowledge how grievous sin is, so our thinking is in line with God's.

All that's left for you to do is to accept the gift that Jesus is holding out for you right now: "If you confess with your mouth, 'Jesus is Lord,' and believe in your heart that God raised him from the dead, you will be saved. For it is with your heart that you believe and are justified, and it is with your mouth that you confess and are saved" (Romans 10:9–10). God says that if you believe in His son, Jesus, you can live forever with Him in glory: "For God so loved the world that He gave his one and only Son, that whoever believes in him shall not perish, but have eternal life" (John 3:16).

Are you ready to accept the gift of eternal life that Jesus is offering you right now? Let's review what this commitment involves:

- I acknowledge I am a sinner in need of a Savior. I repent or turn away from my sin.
- I believe in my heart that God raised Jesus from the dead. I trust that Jesus paid the full penalty for my sins.
- I confess Jesus as my Lord and my God. I surrender control of my life to Jesus.
- I receive Jesus as my Savior forever. I accept that God has done for me and in me what He promised.

If it is your sincere desire to receive Jesus into your heart as your personal Lord and Savior, then talk to God from your heart. Here's a suggested prayer:

Lord Jesus, I know that I am a sinner and I do not deserve eternal life. But, I believe You died and rose from the grave to make me a new creation and to prepare me to dwell in your presence forever. Jesus, come into my life, take control of my life, forgive my sins and save me. I am now placing my trust in You alone for my salvation and I accept your free gift of eternal life.

If you've prayed this prayer, it's important that you take these three next steps: First, go tell another Christian! Second, get plugged into a local church. Third, begin reading your Bible every day (we suggest starting with the book of John). Welcome to God's forever family!

Endnotes

[1] See Numbers 23:19; Titus 1:2; Matthew 24:35; Psalm 12:6–7; Proverbs 30:5; and Psalm 138:2.

[2] Words of Life Ministries, "Series 16: Study 3 The Reward for Obedience: *www.wordsoflife.co.uk/bible-studies/study-3-the-reward-for-obedience/* (January 26, 2017).

[3] Michael S. Houdmann, "How and when was the Canon of the Bible put together?" Got Questions Online: *www.gotquestions.org/canon-Bible.html.* November 7, 2013.

[4] The reader is encouraged to review these additional resources: Henry Halley, *Halley's Bible Handbook.* (Grand Rapids: Zondervan Publishing House, 1927, 1965); Arthur Maxwell, *Your Bible and You.* (Washington D.C.: Review and Herald Publishing Association, 1959); Merrill Unger, *Unger's Bible Handbook.* (Chicago: Moody Press, 1967).

[5] For example, in 1946 the Dead Sea Scrolls were discovered, which included over 900 manuscripts dating from 408 BC to AD 318. These manuscripts were written mostly on parchment (made of animal hide) but with some written on papyrus. Because these materials are fragile, they have to be kept behind special glass in climate controlled areas.

[6] Josh McDowell, *The New Evidence That Demands a Verdict.* (Nashville: Thomas Nelson Publishers, 1999).

[7] Ibid., p. 38.

[8] Ibid., p. 38.

[9] Most of the 11 verses come from 3 John. See: Norman Geisler and William Nix, *A General Introduction to the Bible.* (Chicago: Moody Press, 1986), p. 430.

[10] Ibid., p. 430.

[11] Theophilus ben Ananus was the High Priest in Jerusalem from AD 37 to 41 and was one of the wealthiest and most influential Jewish families in Iudaea Province during the 1st century. He was also the brother-in-law of Joseph Caiaphas, the High Priest before whom Jesus appeared. See Wikipedia and B. Cooper, *The Authenticity of the Book of Genesis.* (Portsmouth, UK: Creation Science Movement, 2012).

[12] Ken Curtis, "Whatever Happened to the Twelve Apostles?" Christianity.com: *www.christianity.com/church/church-history/timeline/1-300/whatever-happened-to-the-twelve-apostles-11629558.html* (January 30, 2017).

[13] B. Cooper, *Authenticity of the New Testament, Vol. 1: The Gospels.* Electronic book (2013).

[14] The Digital Dead Sea Scrolls Online, Directory of Qumran Dead Sea Scroll: *www://dss.collections.imj.org.il/isaiah.* (December 10, 2013).

[15] Source for DSS: Fred Mille, "Qumran Great Isaiah Scroll," Great Isaiah Scroll: *http://www.moellerhaus.com/qumdir.htm*; Source for Aleppo Codes JPS: "Mechon Mamre" (Hebrew for Mamre Institute): *http://www.mechon-mamre.org/p/pt/pt1053.htm.* (December 10, 2013).

[16] Geisler & Nix. *A General Introduction to the Bible.*

[17] Samuel Davidson, *Hebrew Text of the Old Testament,* 2d ed. (London: Samuel Bagster & Sons, 1859), p. 89.

[18] Mary Fairchild, "44 Prophecies of the Messiah Fulfilled in Jesus Christ," About.com: *www.christianity.about.com/od/biblefactsandlists/a/Prophecies-Jesus.htm.* (December 18, 2013).

[19] The author would like to thank Kyle Justice and Taylor Guthrie for reviewing and commenting on this chapter.

[20] See 2 Peter 1:31; 2 Timothy 3:16; Numbers 23:19; Titus 1:2; Matthew 24:35; Psalm 12:6–7; Proverbs 30:5; and Psalm 138:2.

[21] The Biblical timelines that rely on the 17th-century chronology formulated by Bishop James Ussher place Creation at 4004 BC and the Flood at 2348 BC. Some recent research into the copyist differences in the early Masoretic and early Septuagint texts would place the Flood around 2518 BC based on the Masoretic text and 3168 BC based on the Septuagint text. These differences, however, can be settled by comparing multiple texts to reveal the perfect nature of the original writings which were "written through man by God" without error. See: Brian Thomas, "Two date range options for Noah's Flood." *Journal of Creation.* 31(1) (2017); Henry B. Smith Jr., "Methuselah's Begetting Age in Genesis 5:25 and the Primeval Chronology of the Septuagint: A Closer Look at the Textual and Historical Evidence." *Answers Research Journal.* 10 (2017): 169–179 (available: *www.answersingenesis.org/arj/v10/methuselah-primeval-chronology-septuagint.pdf*); and Lita Cosner and Robert Carter, "Textual Traditions and Biblical Chronology," *Journal of Creation.* 29 (2) 2015 (available: *https://creation.com/images/pdfs/tj/j29_2/j29_2_99-105.pdf*).

[22] J. C. Sanford, 2008. *Genetic Entropy and the Mystery of the Genome*, 3rd ed. (Waterloo, NY: FMS Publications).

[23] Encouragement for Believers - Science Update, "Good science affirms Scripture!" *www.logosra.org/genetic-entropy* (January 26, 2017)

[24] Leading Progressive Creationist, Dr. Hugh Ross, places the emergence of the human race via Adam and Eve about 50,000 years ago: Fazale Rana with Hugh Ross, *Who Was Adam?* (Colorado Springs, CO: NavPress, 2005), p. 45. See also: *www.reasons.org/articles/new-date-for-first-aussies* (January 26, 2017)

[25] God Himself provided the light source on day one.

[26] Kenneth R. Miller and Joseph S. Levine, *Biology.* (Boston, MA.: Pearson, 2006), p. 466.

[27] This section was written by Roger Sigler and was carried over from: Daniel A. Biddle (editor), *Creation V. Evolution: What They Won't Tell You in Biology Class* (Xulon Press). Roger Sigler, M.S. is a licensed professional geoscientist in the State of Texas and has taught and published in the field of Biblical Creation since 1989.

[28] Gunter Faure, *Principles of Isotope Geology,* 2nd ed. (John Wiley & Sons, 1986), 41, 119, 288.

[29] A.O.Woodford, *Historical Geology.* (W.H. Freeman and Company, 1965), 191–220.

[30] Judah Etinger, *Foolish Faith.* (Green Forest, AR.: Master Books, 2003), Chapter 3.

[31] C.S. Noble and J.J. Naughton, *Science,* 162 (1968): 265–266.

[32] Data compiled and modified after Snelling (1998): Andrew Snelling, "The Cause of Anomalous Potassium-Argon 'Ages' for Recent Andesite Flows at Mt. Ngauruhoe, New Zealand, and the Implications for Potassium-argon Dating," in Robert E. Walsh (ed.), *Proceedings of the Fourth International Conference on Creationism* (1998), p. 503–525. See also: Andrew A Snelling, "Excess Argon": The "Archilles' Heel" of Potassium-Argon and Argon-Argon "Dating" of Volcanic Rocks. *www.icr.org/article/excess-argon-achillies-heel-potassium-argon-dating/.* (February 3, 2016); Steve Austin, "Excess argon within mineral concentrates from the new dacite lava dome at Mount St Helens volcano," *J. Creation* 10 (3) (1996): 335–343. *www.creation.com/lavadome.* (February 3, 2016).

[33] Andrew Snelling, "Radiocarbon Ages for Fossil Ammonites and Wood in Cretaceous Strata near Redding, California." *Answers Research Journal.* 2008 1: 123-144. *www.answersingenesis.org/geology/carbon-14/radiocarbon-ages-fossils-cretaceous-strata-redding-california/.* (February 3, 2016).

[34] Ibid.

[35] See Paul Giem, Carbon-14 Content of Fossil Carbon, *Origins* 51 (2001): 6-30; J. Baumgardner, Andre Snelling, D.R. Humphreys, and Steve Austin, Measurable 14C in Fossilized Organic Materials: Confirming the Young Earth Creation-Flood Model. In Ivey, H (editor) *Proceedings of the Fifth International Conference on Creationism*, 2003, 127–142. Pittsburgh, PA: Creation Science Fellowship (see also: *www.icr.org/article/young-earth-creation-flood-14c/*); J. Baumgardner, 14C evidence for a recent global flood and a young earth. In Vardiman, L., Snelling, A.A. and Chaffin, E.F. (editors), Radioisotopes and the Age of the Earth: Results of a Young-Earth Creationist Research Initiative, 2005, pp. 587-630. (El Cajon, CA: Institute for Creation Research and Chino Valley, AZ: Creation Research Society). (See also: *www.icr.org/article/carbon-14-evidence-for-recent-global*).

[36] G. Faure, *Principles of Isotope Geology*, 2nd ed., (New York: John Wiley & Sons, 1986), 391.

[37] K. J. Heckman, H. Campbell, H. Powers, B. Law, C. Swanston. "The influence of fire on the radiocarbon signature and character of soil organic matter in the Siskiyou National Forest, Oregon, USA." *Fire Ecology* 9 (2) (2013): 40–56.

[38] Robert Krulwich, "How A-Bomb Testing Changed Our Trees." August 25, 2010 (*www.npr.org/templates/story/story.php?storyId=96750869*) (February 3, 2016).

[39] Image Credit: Wikipedia: *www://en.wikipedia.org/wiki/Radiocarbon_dating#/media/File:Radiocarbon _bomb_spike.svg* (January 26, 2017)

[40] Sheridan Bowman, *Radiocarbon Dating*. (London: British Museum Press, 1995), p. 24–27.

[41] Tree ring dating (dendrochronology) has been used in an attempt to extend the calibration of carbon-14 dating earlier than historical records allow, but this depends on *temporal placement of fragments of wood from trees that have been dead for ages* using carbon-14 dating. For example, the Bristlecone Pines in California were dated to be 4,723 years old by counting the tree rings, which apparently pre-dates Noah's Flood by a few hundred years. However, research conducted on the *same type of tree* shows that seasonal effects can cause multiple rings (up to five) to grow in the same year. It is likely that the world following the Flood would have been much wetter with fewer contrasting seasons until after the Ice Age, which could explain the apparent date of the tree based on counting its rings. When scientists build calibration models for radiocarbon dating that extend back many thousands of years, they attempt to build tree ring chronologies by *"cross-matching" tree ring patterns of pieces of dead wood found near living trees*. This process relies on circular reasoning because it assumes that the "carbon clock" can be moved backwards in time in a straight line, and the Flood greatly disrupted carbon ratios in the earth, as well as the atmosphere that produces the ratios of radioactive and stable carbon. Carbon dating today assumes that the system has been in equilibrium for many thousands of years. However, the Flood buried large quantities of organic matter containing stable carbon (^{12}C) changing the $^{14}C/^{12}C$ ratios. Further, tree ring patterns are not unique (like fingerprints). Dr. Batten (Batten, Don. "Tree ring dating (dendrochronology)." Creation.com. *www.creation.com/tree-ring-dating-dendrochronology*. (February 10, 2016): "There are many points in a given sequence where a sequence from a new piece of wood matches well (note that even two trees growing next to each other will not have identical growth ring patterns). D.K. Yamaguchi, "Interpretation of cross-correlation between tree-ring series." *Tree Ring Bulletin*, 46 (1986): 47–54: Yamaguchi recognized that ring pattern matches are not unique.

178

The best match (using statistical tests) is often rejected in favor of a less exact match because the best match is deemed to be 'incorrect' (particularly if it is too far away from the carbon-14 'age'). So the carbon 'date' is used to constrain just which match is acceptable. Consequently, the calibration is a circular process and the tree ring chronology extension is also a circular process that is dependent on assumptions about the carbon dating system (see: Newgrosh, B., "Living with radiocarbon dates: a response to Mike Baillie." *Journal of the Ancient Chronology Forum* 5:59–67, 1992.).

[42] G. Faure, *Principles of Isotope Geology*, 2nd ed. (New York: John Wiley & Sons, 1986), p. 391; Ken Ham, Andrew Snelling, and Carl Weiland, *The Answers Book*, (El Cajon, CA.: Master Books), 1992, p. 68.

[43] F. Miyake, K. Nagaya, K. Masuda, T. Nakamura, "A signature of cosmic-ray increase in AD 774–775 from tree rings in Japan," *Nature* 486 (7402) (2012): 240–242.

[44] I.G. Usoskin, "The AD 775 cosmic event revisited: The Sun is to blame," *Astronomy & Astrophysics* 552 (1) (2013): L3.

[45] Minze Stuiver, "Variations in Radiocarbon Concentration and Sunspot Activity," *J. Geophysical Research* 66 (1961): 273-76.

[46] R.E. Taylor and O. Bar-Yosef. *Radiocarbon Dating: An Archaeological Perspective*, 2nd Ed. (Left Coast Press, Walnut Creek, CA, 2014), pp. 31–32; 150–155.

[47] Ibid., 45–46.

[48] J. Baumgardner, "14C evidence for a recent global flood and a young earth." In L. Vardiman, Andrew Snelling, and E.F. Chaffin (editors), *Radioisotopes and the Age of the Earth: Results of a Young-Earth Creationist Research Initiative.* (El Cajon, CA: Institute for Creation Research and Chino Valley, AZ, 2005), p. 618. Creation Research Society. (*www.icr.org/article/carbon-14-evidence-for-recent-global*) (January 26, 2017)

[49] Brian Thomas and Vance Nelson, "Radiocarbon in Dinosaur and Other Fossils," *Creation Research Society Quarterly*, 51 (4) (2015): 299–311.

[50] Charles Foley, "Dating the Shroud," *The Tablet: International Catholic News Weekly*, (July 7, 1990): 13.

[51] There are "dragon" legends in almost every culture in the world; ancient drawing and carvings of dinosaur-like creatures in almost every continent; and even several dragon/dinosaur accounts from several credible historians around the world—historians that are regarded as authorities in other areas, but whose accounts regarding dragons are dismissed by those holding to the older earth viewpoint. The reader is encouraged to draw from the resources at *www.answersingenesis.org* for books that discuss this area thoroughly.

[52] Image credit: *www.dinopedia.wikia.com* (January 26, 2017).

[53] While no expert really knows for sure how Triceratops' used their horns, many ideas have been proposed: Andrew A. Farke, 2004. "Horn Use in

Triceratops (Dinosauria: Ceratopsidae): Testing Behavioral Hypotheses Using Scale Models." Palaeontologia Electronica 7(1):10, p. 3.

[54] J. Scannella and Jack Horner (2010) "Torosaurus Marsh, 1891 is Triceratops, Marsh, 1889 (Ceratopsidae: Chasmosaurinae) synonymy through ontogeny." *Journal of Vertebrate Paleontology* 30: 1157–1168.

[55] G.S. Paul and P. Christiansen, 2000. "Forelimb posture in neoceratopsian dinosaurs: Implications for gait and locomotion." *Paleobiology*, 26(3):450-465.

[56] Image credit: Wikipedia.

[57] Image credit: Shutterstock.

[58] Scannella & Horner (2010).

[59] An early reconstruction by Gregory S. Paul estimated Argentinosaurus at between 30–35 meters (98–115 ft.) in length and with a weight of up to 80–100 tonnes (88–110 short tons). The length of the skeletal restoration mounted in Museo Carmen Funes is 39.7 meters (130 ft.) long and 7.3 meters (24 ft.) high. This is the longest reconstruction in a museum and contains the original material, including a mostly complete fibula. Other estimates place the creature at 115 feet long and between 165,000 and 220,000 pounds (*www.bbc.co.uk/nature/life/Argentinosaurus*) (January 26, 2017).

[60] Image credit: Wikipedia.

[61] Carl Werner, *Living Fossils, Evolution: The Grand Experiment*, vol 1. (Green Forest, AR: New Leaf Press, 2009).

[62] "Fast Facts about the Bible." Bibleresources.org: *www.bibleresources.org/bibleresources/bible-facts/* (January 26, 2017)

[63] M. P. Taylor and M. J. Wedel. "Why sauropods had long necks; and why giraffes have short necks." *PeerJ* 1: (2013), e36.

[64] Image Credit: Wikipedia (*www://en.wikipedia.org/wiki/Mamenchisaurus*) (January 26, 2017).

[65] M.J. Wedel, "Aligerando a los gigantes (Lightening the giants)." *¡Fundamental!* 2007, 12:1–84. [in Spanish, with English translation]

[66] See also: "Mechanical implications of pneumatic neck vertebrae in sauropod dinosaurs." Daniela Schwarz-Wings, Christian A. Meyer, Eberhard Frey, Hans-Rudolf Manz-Steiner, Ralf Schumacher *Proc. R. Soc. B* 2010 277 11–17.

[67] Wedel, 2007.

[68] University of California Museum of Paleontology, Matt Wedel: Hunting the inflatable dinosaur *www.ucmp.berkeley.edu/science/profiles/wedel_0609.php* (January 26, 2017).

[69] Taylor & Wedel, 2013.

[70] Taylor & Wedel, 2013.

[71] Different types of sauropods had more or fewer vertebrae.

[72] David Catchpoole, Grass-eating dinos: A 'time-travel' problem for evolution (www.creation.com/grass-eating-dinos) (August 22, 2017); Brian Thomas, Dinosaurs Ate Rice, *www.icr.org/article/6428/* (August 22, 2017).

[73] Nicole Klein, Kristian Remes, Carole T. Gee, and P. Martin Sander, Biology of the Sauropod Dinosaurs Understanding the Life of Giants (Indiana University Press, 2011).

[74] M. Hallett & M. Wedel, *The Sauropod Dinosaurs: Life in the Age of Giants,* (Johns Hopkins University Press, 2016).

[75] Patrick Moser, Jordan River could die by 2011, Phys Org. *www.phys.org/news/2010-05-jordan-river-die.html* (May 2, 2010) (August 22, 2017).

[76] See, for example, the English Standard Version or the Life Application Study Bible notes.

[77] J. Carballido, D. Pol, A. Otero, I. Cerda, L. Salgado, A. Garrido, J. Ramezani, N. Cúneo, M. Krause, A new giant titanosaur sheds light on body mass evolution amongst sauropod dinosaurs, *Proceedings of the Royal Society B* (August 9, 2017).

[78] Nathan P. Myhrvold and Philip J. Currie, Supersonic Sauropods? Tail Dynamics in the Diplodocids, *Paleobiology* 23 (December, 1997): 393—409; Benjamin Meyers, W. Wayt Gibbs, Did a Dinosaur Break the Sound Barrier before We Did? (*www.scientificamerican.com/video/did-a-dinosaur-break-the-sound-barrier-before-we-did/*) (November 3, 2015) (August 22, 2017).

[79] Dattatreya Mandal, *Hexapolis*, Physical Model To Show How Dinosaurs May Have Whipped Their Tails In Supersonic Speed (October 16, 2015). (www.hexapolis.com/2015/10/16/physical-model-to-show-how-dinosaurs-may-have-whipped-their-tails-in-supersonic-speed/) (August 23, 2017).

[80] David Lambert, *The Encyclopedia of Dinosaurs* (London: Bloomsbury Books, 1994), p. 26–27, published in association with the British Museum of Natural History. Reconstructed graphic provided by Dr. Tommy Mitchell, Answers in Genesis.

[81] Carl Werner, *Evolution: The Grand Experiment* (3rd Edition). New Leaf Press. Kindle Edition. (Kindle Locations 1473-1476)

[82] Werner, p. 116

[83] Werner, Kindle Locations 2597-2599).

[84] Most Biblical creationists hold that some dinosaurs lived after the Flood, but the vast majority of these likely went extinct rather quickly for a multitude of reasons.

[85] Peter D. Ward, *Out of Thin Air: Dinosaurs, Birds, and Earth's Ancient Atmosphere.* (Washington, DC: Joseph Henry Press, 2006).

[86] See 2 Peter 3:6; Genesis 1; and Romans 8:22.

[87] See Romans 5:12 and 1 Corinthians 15:22.

[88] Dr. Andrew A. Snelling, "Noah's Lost World," 2014; last featured May 3, 2015 (*https://answersingenesis.org/geology/plate-tectonics/noahs-lost-world/*) (January 26, 2017).

[89] *The New Defender Study Bible* (Nashville, TN: World Publishing, 2006) states, "9:13 my bow. The rainbow, requiring small water droplets in the air, could not form in the pre-diluvian world, where the high vapor canopy precluded rain (Genesis 2:5). After the Flood, the very fact that rainfall is now possible makes a worldwide rainstorm impossible, and the rainbow "in the cloud" thereby becomes a perpetual reminder of God's grace, even in judgment." Several other Biblical Creation resources hold this view.

[90] Catherine Brahic, *New Scientist Daily News* (April 24, 2007). "Mystery prehistoric fossil verified as giant fungus": (*www.newscientist.com/article/dn11701-mystery-prehistoric-fossil-verified-as-giant-fungus/#.Uea7Qo2G18E*) (January 26, 2017).

[91] Image Credit: Shutterstock.

[92] It is commonly taught in evolution-based textbooks that the oxygen levels during the "Carboniferous" era were 35%. See, for example: David Beerling, *The emerald planet: how plants changed Earth's history.* (Oxford University Press, 2007), 47. Peter D. Ward, *Out of Thin Air: Dinosaurs, Birds, and Earth's Ancient Atmosphere*, (Washington, DC: Joseph Henry Press, 2006), Chapter 6. See also: R. A. Berner, D. J. Beerling, R. Dudley, J.M. Robinson, R.A Wildman, Jr. "Phanerozoic atmospheric oxygen." *Annual Review Earth Planet Science*, 2003, pp. 31, 105–134.

[93] Jeff Hecht, November 6, 1993, "Last gasp for the dinosaurs." *New Scientist.* www.newscientist.com/article/mg14018981-200-last-gasp-for-the-dinosaurs/ (January 26, 2017).

[94] *The Washington Post.* "Lack of Oxygen Blamed for Dinosaurs' Extinction." October 28, 1993 *www.washingtonpost.com/archive/politics/1993/10/28/lack-of-oxygen-blamed-for-dinosaurs-extinction/84f102be-4264-4089-9e10-007b181476ee/?utm_term=.333d8cd2fefb* (January 26, 2017). See also: R. A. Hengst, J. K. Rigby, G. P. Landis, R. L. Sloan. "Biological consequences of Mesozoic atmospheres: respiratory adaptations and functional range of Apatosaurus." In: Macleod N, Keller G, editors. *Cretaceous-Tertiary mass extinctions: biotic and environmental changes.* (New York: W.W. Norton & Co., 1996), pp. 327–347.

[95] Carl Wieland and Dr Jonathan Sarfati, "Some bugs do grow bigger with higher oxygen," *Journal of Creation* 25(1):13–14 (April 2011) (*http://creation.com/oxygen-bigger-bugs*) (January 26, 2017). See also J. Scheven, "The Carboniferous floating forest—an extinct pre-Flood ecosystem," *J. Creation* 10 (1):70–91, 1996.

[96] *Guinness World Book of Records 2014,* (The Jim Pattison Group, 2014), 27.

[97] Image Credit: Wikipedia.

[98] Gregory S. Paul, *Dinosaurs of the Air: The Evolution and Loss of Flight in Dinosaurs and Birds* (Johns Hopkins University Press, 2002), 472. See also: M.P. Witton and M.B. Habib. "On the Size and Flight Diversity of Giant Pterosaurs, the Use of Birds as Pterosaur Analogues and Comments on Pterosaur Flightlessness." *PLoS ONE,* 5(11) (2010). Other estimates place a range the weight range between 440 and 570 pounds: "That said, most mass estimates for the largest pterosaurs do converge, using multiple methods, around a 200–260kg [440–570lb] range at present, which represents decent confidence." (Ella Davies, BBC Earth, May 9, 2016) and "The biggest beast that ever flew had wings longer than a bus." (*www.bbc.com/earth/story/20160506-the-biggest-animals-that-ever-flew-are-long-extinct*) (January 26, 2017).

[99] Larry O' Hanlon, November 8, 2012. "This pterodactyl was so big it couldn't fly, scientist claims." *www.nbcnews.com/id/49746642/ns/technology_and_science-science/#.WH-U2_krKUn* (January 26, 2017).

[100] Mark P. Wilton, *Pterosaurs: Natural History, Evolution, Anatomy.* (Princeton University Press, 2013).

[101] Oxygen reported from within the amber bubbles are still debated among evolutionists.

[102] Ian Anderson, "Dinosaurs Breathed Air Rich in Oxygen," *New Scientist,* vol. 116, 1987, p. 25.

[103] Image Credit: Wikipedia.

[104] "No giants today: tracheal oxygen supply to the legs limits beetle size," was presented October 10-11 at Comparative Physiology 2006: Integrating Diversity (Virginia Beach). The research was carried out by Alexander Kaiser and Michael C. Quinlan of Midwestern University, Glendale, Arizona; J. Jake Socha and Wah-Keat Lee, Argonne National Laboratory, Argonne, IL; and Jaco Klok and Jon F. Harrison, Arizona State University, Tempe, AZ. Harrison is the principal investigator.

[105] Geological Society of America. "Raising giant insects to unravel ancient oxygen." *Science Daily,* October 30, 2010. *www.sciencedaily.com/releases/2010/10/101029132924.htm* (January 26, 2017). See also: Gauthier Chapelle & Lloyd S. Peck (May 1999). "Polar gigantism dictated by oxygen availability." *Nature.* 399 (6732): 114–115. This article argues that higher oxygen supply (30–35%) may also have led to larger insects during the Carboniferous period: A.N. Nel, G. Fleck, R. Garrouste, and G. Gand, "The Odonatoptera of the Late Permian Lodève Basin (Insecta)." *Journal of Iberian Geology* 34 (1) (2008): 115–122.

[106] Colin Schultz, "Long Before Trees Overtook the Land, Earth Was Covered by Giant Mushrooms," Smithsonian.com (July 17, 2013). *www.smithsonianmag.com/smart-news/long-before-trees-overtook-the-land-earth-was-covered-by-giant-mushrooms-13709647/* (January 26, 2017).

[107] University of Chicago News Office. "Prehistoric mystery organism verified as giant fungus 'Humongous fungus' towered over all life on land" *www-news.uchicago.edu/releases/07/070423.fungus.shtml* (April 23, 2007) (January 26, 2017).

[108] Simon J. Braddy, Markus Poschmann, and O. Erik Tetlie, "Giant claw reveals the largest ever arthropod," *Biological Letters.* (2008) 4 106–109 (Published February 23, 2008).

[109] M. G. Lockley & Christian Meyer. "The tradition of tracking dinosaurs in Europe," *Dinosaur Tracks and Other Fossil Footprints of Europe.* (Columbia University Press, 2013), pp. 25–52. See also: Donald R. Prothero, *Bringing Fossils to Life: An Introduction to Paleobiology.* Third Edition. (New York: Columbia University Press, 2015), p. 381.

[110] ThePaleobiology Database (Frequently Asked Questions): *https://paleobiodb.org/#/faq* (January 26, 2017)

[111] ThePaleobiology Database: *https://paleobiodb.org/navigator/* (January 26, 2017)

[112] RATE tested the assumptions using radiohalos and fission tracks. Both showed that the assumptions were violated (Larry Vardiman, Steven Austin, John Baumgardner, Steven Boyd, Eugene Chaffin, Donald DeYoung, D. Russell Humphreys, Andrew Snelling, *Radioisotopes and the Age of the Earth: Results of a Young-Earth Research Initiative.* The Institute for Creation Research).

[113] Ken Ham, "They Can't Allow 'It'!" AnswersinGenesis.org: *www.answersingenesis.org/articles/au/cant-allow-it* (January 1, 2014).

[114] Blake Edgar, "Dinosaur National Monument." *Dinosaur Digs.* (Bethesda, MD: Discovery Communications, 1999), p. 120.

[115] William A. Hoesch and Steven A. Austin, "Dinosaur National Monument: Jurassic Park Or Jurassic Jumble?" ICR.org: *www.icr.org/article/dinosaur-national-monument-park-or-jurassic-jumble/* (January 27, 2017).

[116] An articulated dinosaur skeleton means that a large number of the bones from an individual dinosaur were collected in close association, enough to reassemble the dinosaur.

[117] Werner, *Evolution: The Grand Experiment*, Kindle Locations 2598–2608).

[118] Other researchers have framed similar explanations about the same area: "It looks like catastrophe… We think a herd was trying to cross a river in flood. These animals weren't too bright." Phillip Currie, quoted in Rick Gore, "Dinosaurs." *National Geographic*, January 1993, p. 46.

184

[119] Werner, *Evolution: The Grand Experiment* (Kindle Locations 2598–2608).

[120] There is disagreement in the paleontology field as to whether the "dinosaur death pose" is due to choking while dying from drowning, or due to strong water currents arching the neck back after death. See: Achim G. Reisdorf & Michael Wuttke, "Re-evaluating Moodie's Opisthotonic-Posture Hypothesis in Fossil Vertebrates Part I: Reptiles—the taphonomy of the bipedal dinosaurs Compsognathus longipes and Juravenator starki from the Solnhofen Archipelago (Jurassic, Germany)," *Palaeobiodiversity and Palaeoenvironments* 92 (2012):119–168. Their findings stated, "From what has been presented above, it can be concluded that the formation of the 'opisthotonic posture' in *subaquatically deposited carcasses* of long-necked and long tailed reptiles is the result of a postmortem process...this posture must be seen as a normal phenomenon that occurs during subaquatic gradual embedding of these sorts of carcasses." See discussion: Drwile.com, "Arched Necks in Dinosaur Fossils: Is Water to Blame?" *www.blog.drwile.com/?p=7118* (February 16, 2016).

[121] D.A. Eberth, D.B. Brinkman, and V.A. Barkas, "Centrosaurine Mega-bonebed from the Upper Cretaceous of Southern Alberta: Implications for Behaviour and Death Events" in *New Perspectives on Horned Dinosaurs: The Ceratopsian Symposium at the Royal Tyrrell Museum* (September 2007).

[122] *New Perspectives on Horned Dinosaurs: The Ceratopsian Symposium at the Royal Tyrrell Museum* (September 2007).

[123] Michael Reilly, "Dinosaurs' Last Stand Found in China?" Discovery.com: *www.news.discovery.com/earth/dinosaurs-last-stand-found-in-china.htm* (January 1, 2014).

[124] Michael J. Oard, "The Extinction of the Dinosaurs," *Journal of Creation* 11(2) (1997): 137–154.

[125] J.R. Horner & J. Gorman, *Digging Dinosaurs*. New York: Workman Publishing, 1988, pp. 122–123.

[126] Credit: Caleb LePore. See: David Maxwell Braun, "Dinosaur Herd Found in Canada Named After Science Teacher." *National Geographic News.* National Geographic Society, October 2, 2008; Christopher A. Brochu, M. K. Brett-Surman. "Dinosaur Provincial Park." *A Guide to Dinosaurs.* (San Francisco, CA: Fog City, 2002), p. 220; John R. Horner and James Gorman. *Digging Dinosaurs.* (New York: Workman Pub., 1988), p. 131; Brett French, "New Finds, Old Site: Dinosaur Dig Revealing Insights into Montana 103 Million Years Ago." *Butte Montana Local News.* (August 23, 2015); Brett French, "Jurassic Starfish Discovery in South-central Montana Wows Researchers." *Independent Record.* (July 6, 2015); Blake Edgar, "Petrified Forest National Park." *Dinosaur Digs.* (Bethesda, MD: Discovery Communications, 1999), p. 104; Glendive Dinosaur and Fossil Museum, Glendive, Montana; Mike Dunham, "Scientists Identify Dinosaur That

Roamed the Alaska Arctic." *Alaska Dispatch News*. Alaska Dispatch Publishing. (September 22, 2015).

[127] Tim Clarey, Ph.D. "Dinosaurs in Marine Sediments: A Worldwide Phenomenon." *Acts & Facts*. 44 (6) (2015).

[128] J. H. Hartman and J. I. Kirkland. "Brackish and marine mollusks of the Hell Creek Formation of North Dakota: Evidence for a persisting Cretaceous seaway." In *The Hell Creek Formation and the Cretaceous-Tertiary Boundary in the Northern Great Plains: An Integrated Continental Record of the End of the Cretaceous*. J. H. Hartman, K. R. Johnson, and D. J. Nichols, eds. Geological Society of America Special Paper 361, pp. 271–296. (2002); W. A. Clemens and J. H. Hartman. "From Tyrannosaurus rex to asteroid impact: Early studies (1901–1980) of the Hell Creek Formation in its type area." In *Through the End of the Cretaceous in the Type Locality of the Hell Creek Formation in Montana and Adjacent Areas*. Wilson, G. P. et al, eds. Geological Society of America Special Paper 503, pp. 1–87. 2014.

[129] Jesse A. Sherburn, John R. Baumgardner and Mark F. Horstemeyer, "New Material Model Reveals Inherent Tendency in Mantle Minerals for Runaway Mantle Dynamics," *International Conference on Creationism* (2013).

[130] N. Ibrahim, et al. 2014. "Semiaquatic adaptations in a giant predatory dinosaur." *Science*. 345 (6204): 1613–1616.

[131] Horner & Gorman, *Digging Dinosaurs*, 128.

[132] Tim Clarey, Ph.D. "Dinosaurs in Marine Sediments: A Worldwide Phenomenon." *Acts & Facts*. 44 (6) (2015).

[133] I am grateful for the review and input on this section from Brian Thomas and Pat Roy.

[134] *Creation Research Society Quarterly Journal* Spring 2015 (Volume 51, Number 4): *www.creationresearch.org/index.php/component/k2/item/118-2015-volume-51-number-4-spring* (January 27, 2017)

[135] Jeff Hecht, Daily News, "Blood vessels recovered from T. rex bone," NewScientist.com: *www.newscientist.com/article/dn7195-blood-vessels-recovered-from-t-rex-bone/* (March 24, 2005)

[136] Science via AP (*www.msnbc.msn.com/id/7285683/*) (January 27, 2017).

[137] See, for example: R. Pawlicki and M. Wowogrodzka-Zagorska. "Blood vessels and red blood cells preserved in dinosaur bones." Annals of Anatomy 180 (1998): 73–77; M. H. Schweitzer, J.L. Wittmeyer, J.R. Horner, and J.K Toporske. "Soft-tissue vessels and cellular preservation in Tyrannosaurus rex." *Science,* 307 (2005): 1952; M.H. Schweitzer, J.L. Wittmeyer, and J.R. Horner. "Soft tissue and cellular preservation in vertebrate skeletal elements from the Cretaceous to the present." *Proceedings of the Royal Society B* 274 (2007): 183–197; M.H. Schweitzer, W. Zheng, C.L. Organ, R. Avci, Z. Suo, L.M. Freimark, V.S. Lebleu, M.B. Duncan, M.G. Vander Heiden, J.M. Neveu, W.S. Lane, J.S. Cottrell, J.R. Horner, L.C. Cantley, R. Kalluri, and

J.M. Asara. "Biomolecular characterization and protein sequences of the campanian Hadrosaur B. Canadensis." *Science*, 324 (2009): 626–631.
[138] M. Schweitzer and I. Staedter, *The Real Jurassic Park, Earth*, June 1997, pp. 55–57.
[139] R. Pawlicki and M. Wowogrodzka-Zagorska. "Blood vessels and red blood cells preserved in dinosaur bones." *Annals of Anatomy* 180 (1998): 73–77; M. H. Schweitzer, J.L. Wittmeyer, J.R. Horner, and J.K Toporske. "Soft-tissue vessels and cellular preservation in Tyrannosaurus rex." *Science,* 307 (2005): 1952; M.H. Schweitzer, J.L. Wittmeyer, and J.R. Horner. "Soft tissue and cellular preservation in vertebrate skeletal elements from the Cretaceous to the present." *Proceedings of the Royal Society B* 274 (2007): 183–197; M.H. Schweitzer, W. Zheng, C.L. Organ, R. Avci, Z. Suo, L.M. Freimark, V.S. Lebleu, M.B. Duncan, M.G. Vander Heiden, J.M. Neveu, W.S. Lane, J.S. Cottrell, J.R. Horner, L.C. Cantley, R. Kalluri, and J.M. Asara. "Biomolecular characterization and protein sequences of the campanian Hadrosaur B. Canadensis." *Science* 324 (2009): 626–631; J. Lindgren, M.W. Caldwell, T. Konishi, L.M. Chiappe, "Convergent Evolution in Aquatic Tetrapods: Insights from an Exceptional Fossil Mosasaur." *PLoS ONE* 5(8) (2010): e11998.
[140] Barry Yeoman, "Schweitzer's Dangerous Discovery," Discovery Magazine: www.discovermagazine.com/2006/apr/dinosaur-dna (April 27, 2006) (January 27, 2017).
[141] M.H. Schweitzer, M. Marhsall, K. Carron, D.S. Bohle, S.C. Busse, E.V. Arnold, D. Barnard, J.R. Horner, and J.R. Starkey. "Heme compounds in dinosaur trabecular bone." *Proceedings of the National Academy of Sciences* USA 94, (1997), p. 6295.
[142] J.M. Asara, M.H. Schweitzer, L.M. Freimark, M. Phillips, and L.C. Cantley. "Protein sequences from mastodon and Tyrannosaurus rex revealed by mass spectrometry." *Science*, 316 (2007): 280–285.
[143] M. Armitage, "Soft bone material from a brow horn of a Triceratops horridus from Hell Creek Formation, MT." *Creation Research Society Quarterly,* 51 (2015): 248–258.
[144] M.H. Schweitzer, W. Zheng, T.P. Cleland, and M. Bern. "Molecular analyses of dinosaur osteocytes support the presence of endogenous molecules." *Bone*, 52 (2013): 414–423; M. Armitage, "Soft bone material from a brow horn of a Triceratops horridus from Hell Creek Formation, MT." *Creation Research Society Quarterly,* 51 (2015): 248–258; M. Armitage and K.L. Anderson. "Soft tissue of fibrillar bone from a fossil of the supraorbital horn of the dinosaur Triceratops horridus." *Acta Histochemica*, 115 (2013):603–608; R. Pawlicki, "Histochemical demonstration of DNA in osteocytes from dinosaur bones." *Folia Histochemica Et Cytobiologica*, 33 (1995): 183–186.

187

[145] M.H. Schweitzer, et al. 2005. "Molecular preservation in Late Cretaceous sauropod dinosaur eggshells." *Proceedings of the Royal Society B: Biological Sciences.* 272 (1565): 775–784.

[146] G.D. Cody, N.S. Gupta, D.E.G. Briggs, A.L.D. Kilcoyne, R.E. Summons, F. Kenig, R.E. Plotnick, and A. C. Scott. "Molecular signature of chitin-protein complex in Paleozoic arthropods." *Geology,* 39 (3) (2011): 255–258; H. Ehrlich, J.K. Rigby, J.P. Botting, M.V. Tsurkan, C. Werner, P. Schwille, Z. Petrášek, A. Pisera, P. Simon, V.N. Sivkov, D.V. Vyalikh, S.L. Molodtsov, D. Kurek, M. Kammer, S. Hunoldt, R. Born, D. Stawski, A. Steinhof, V.V. Bazhenov, and T. Geisler. "Discovery of 505-million-year old chitin in the basal demosponge Vauxia gracilenta." *Scientific Reports.* 3 (2013): 3497.

[147] M. Helder, "Fresh dinosaur bones found," *Creation* 14(3) (1992): 16–17, *www.creation.com/fresh-dinosaur-bones-found* (January 27, 2017).

[148] "Fossils of new duck-billed, plant-eating dinosaur species found in Alaska, researchers say." *www.accesswdun.com/article/2015/9/337248* (September 22, 2015).

[149] M.H. Schweitzer, J.L. Wittmeyer, and J.R. Horner. "Soft tissue and cellular preservation in vertebrate skeletal elements from the Cretaceous to the present." *Proceedings of the Royal Society B,* 274 (2007):183–197.

[150] Hirotsugu Mori, Patrick S. Druckenmiller, and Gregory M. Erickson, "A new Arctic hadrosaurid from the Prince Creek Formation (lower Maastrichtian) of northern Alaska." *Acta Palaeontologica Polonica* 61 (1), (2016): 15–32; A.R. Fiorillo, P.J. McCarthy, and P.P. Flaig "Taphonomic and sedimentologic interpretations of the dinosaur-bearing Upper Cretaceous Strata of the Prince Creek Formation, Northern Alaska: Insights from an ancient high-latitude terrestrial ecosystem." *Palaeogeography, Palaeoclimatology, Palaeoecology* 295 (2010): 376–388; R.A. Gangloff and A.R. Fiorillo, "Taphonomy and paleoecology of a bonebed from the Prince Creek Formation, North Slope, Alaska." *Palaios*, 25 (2010): 299–317; M.H. Schweitzer, C. Johnson, T.G. Zocco, J.R. Horner, and J.R. Starkey, "Preservation of biomolecules in cancellous bone of Tyrannosaurus rex," *J. Vertebrate paleontology* 17 (2) (1997): 349–359; M.H. Schweitzer, M. Marshall, K. Carron, D.S. Bohle, S.C. Busse, E.V. Arnold, D. Barnard, J.R. Horner, and J.R. Starkey, "Heme compounds in dinosaur trabecular bone," *Proceedings of the National Academy of Science* 94 (1997): 6291–6296; As stated in Helder (above): "An initial announcement was printed in 1985 in Geological Society of America abstract programs Vol.17, p. 548. Already in press at that time was an article describing the site and the condition of the bones (Kyle L. Davies, 'Duck-bill Dinosaurs (Hadrosauridae, Ornithischia) from the North Slope of Alaska', Journal of Paleontology, Vol.61 No.1, pp.198-200); M.H. Schweitzer, J.L. Wittmeyer, and J.R. Horner. "Soft tissue and cellular preservation in vertebrate skeletal

elements from the Cretaceous to the present." *Proceedings of the Royal Society B,* 274 (2007): 183–197.

[151] Barry Yeoman, "Schweitzer's Dangerous Discovery," Discovery Magazine: *www.discovermagazine.com/2006/apr/dinosaur-dna* (April 27, 2006) (January 27, 2017).

[152] Severo Avila, "Alan Stout is the Bone Collector," Northwest Georgia News: *www.northwestgeorgianews.com/rome/lifestyles/alan-stout-is-the-bone-collector/article_6b1268e7-3350-5dfd-a3dc-652dcf27d174.html* (April 11, 2010) (January 27, 2017).

[153] Alan Stout, Personal communication, January 16, 2017.

[154] Marshall Bern, Brett S. Phinney, and David Goldberg. "Reanalysis of Tyrannosaurus Rex Mass Spectra." *Journal of Proteome Research* 8.9 (2009): 4328–4332.

[155] Brian Thomas, "Original Biomaterials in Fossils." *Creation Research Society Quarterly*, 51 (2015): 234–347.

[156] Elena R. Schroeter, Caroline J. DeHart, Timothy P. Cleland, Wenxia Zheng, Paul M. Thomas, Neil L. Kelleher, Marshall Bern, and Mary H. Schweitzer, "Expansion for the Brachylophosaurus canadensis Collagen I Sequence and Additional Evidence of the Preservation of Cretaceous Protein." Journal of Proteome Research Article.

[157] See UPI News: *www.upi.com/Science_News/2017/01/23/Scientists-find-ancient-dinosaur-collagen/6091485202598/* (January 23, 2017).

[158] S. Bertazzo, et al. "Fibres and cellular structures preserved in 75-million-year-old dinosaur specimens," *Nature Communications*, 6, (2015).

[159] M. Buckley and M.J. Collins. "Collagen survival and its use for species identification in Holocene-Lower Pleistocene bone fragments from British archaeological and paleontological sites." *Antiqua*, 1 (2011): e1. Hypothetically, if dinosaurs include an unrealistically large mass of initial collagen, it may last as long as 1.7 million years (see Brian Thomas, "A Review of Original Tissue Fossils and their Age Implications," Proceedings of the Seventh International Conference on Creationism [Pittsburgh, PA: Creation Science Fellowship]). However, this upper estimate assumes that skin, muscles, and connective tissue collagen decays as slowly as bone collagen, which is not typically the case (Brian Thomas, personal communication, February 15, 2017).

[160] Robert F. Service, "Scientists retrieve 80-million-year-old dinosaur protein in 'milestone' paper," Science.com: *www.sciencemag.org/news/2017/01/scientists-retrieve-80-million-year-old-dinosaur-protein-milestone-paper* (January 31, 2017) (February 5, 2017).

[161] M. H. Schweitzer, et al. "Molecular analyses of dinosaur osteocytes support the presence of endogenous molecules." *Bone*, 52 (1) (2013): 414–423. S. R. Woodward, N. J. Weyand, and M. Bunnell. "DNA Sequence from Cretaceous Period Bone Fragments." *Science*, 266 (5188) (1994): 1229–1232.

[162] T. Lingham-Soliar, "A unique cross section through the skin of the dinosaur Psittacosaurus from China showing a complex fibre architecture." *Proceedings of the Royal Society B: Biological Sciences* 275 (2008): 775–780;

T. Lingham-Soliar and G. Plodowski. "The integument of Psittacosaurus from Liaoning Province, China: taphonomy, epidermal patterns and color of a ceratopsian dinosaur." *Naturwissenschaften* 97 (2010): 479–486.

[163] M.H. Schweitzer, W. Zheng, T.P. Cleland, and M. Bern. Molecular analyses of dinosaur osteocytes support the presence of endogenous molecules. *Bone,* 52 (2013): 414–423.

[164] Ibid.

[165] N.P. Edwards, H.E. Barden, B.E. van Dongen, P.L. Manning, P.O. Larson, U. Bergmann, W.I. Sellers, and R.A. Wogelius. "Infrared mapping resolves soft tissue preservation in 50 million year-old reptile skin." *Proceedings of the Royal Society B,* 278 (2011): 3209–3218.

[166] U. Bergmann, et al., "Archaeopteryx feathers and bone chemistry fully revealed via synchrotron imaging." *Proceedings of the National Academy of Sciences.* 107 (20) (2010), 9060–9065.

[167] S. Hayashi, K. Carpenter, M. Watabe, and L.A. McWhinney, "Ontogenetic histology of Stegosaurus plates and spikes." *Palaeontology* 55 (2012), 145–161.

[168] M.H. Schweitzer, W. Zheng, C.L. Organ, R. Avci, Z. Suo, L.M. Freimark, V.S. Lebleu, M.B. Duncan, M.G. Vander Heiden, J.M. Neveu, W.S. Lane, J.S. Cottrell, J.R. Horner, L.C. Cantley, R. Kalluri, and J.M. Asara. "Biomolecular characterization and protein sequences of the campanian Hadrosaur B. Canadensis." *Science,* 324 (2009): 626–631.

[169] M. Buckley and M.J. Collins. "Collagen survival and its use for species identification in Holocene-Lower Pleistocene bone fragments from British archaeological and paleontological sites." *Antiqua,* 1 (2011): e1. Hypothetically, if dinosaurs include an unrealistically large mass of initial collagen, it may last as long as 1.7 million years (see Brian Thomas, "A Review of Original Tissue Fossils and their Age Implications," Proceedings of the Seventh International Conference on Creationism [Pittsburgh, PA: Creation Science Fellowship]). However, this upper estimate assumes that skin, muscles, and connective tissue collagen decays as slowly as bone collagen, which is not typically the case (Brian Thomas, personal communication, February 15, 2017).

[170] *Creation Research Society Quarterly Journal,* Spring 2015 (Volume 51, Number 4): *www.creationresearch.org/index.php/component/k2/item/118-2015-volume-51-number-4-spring* (January 27, 2017).

[171] Image Credit: Wikipedia: *www.commons.wikimedia.org/wiki/File:Edmontosaurus_mummy.jpg*

[172] Image Credit: Wikipedia: *www.news.nationalgeographic.com/news/2002/10/1010_021010_dinomummy.html*

[173] Image Credit: Dinosaur Mummy: *www.dinosaurmummy.org/guide-to-dinosaur-mummy-csi.html*

[174] Image Credit: Wikipedia: https://upload.wikimedia.org/wikipedia/commons/thumb/2/28/Leonardo_mummified_brachylophosaurus.jpg/1280px-Leonardo_mummified_brachylophosaurus.jpg

[175] Michael Greshko, "Hearts of Stone: A Fabulous Fossil Find," National Geographic: *http://news.nationalgeographic.com/2016/04/160421-fossils-hearts-fish-evolution-paleontology-science/* (April 21, 2016) (January 27, 2017).

[176] Nicholas St. Fleur, "First Fossilized Dinosaur Brain Found." New York Times: *www.nytimes.com/2016/10/28/science/first-fossilized-dinosaur-brain.html?_r=0* (October 27, 2016) (January 27, 2017).

[177] Image Credit: *www.ox.ac.uk/news/2016-10-28-fossilised-dinosaur-brain-tissue-identified-first-time* (January 27, 2017)

[178] The author pre-supposes the truth and accuracy of Scripture.

[179] Ian Tattersall, the Director of the American Museum of Natural History: "You could fit it all into the back of a pickup truck if you didn't mind how much you jumbled everything up." Bill Bryson, *A Short History of Nearly Everything* (London: Black Swan Publishing, 2004), 529.

[180] *Nature* Volume 274, #4419 (July 10, 1954): 61–62.

[181] Pat Shipman, "On the Trail of the Piltdown Fraudsters," *New Scientist*, 128 (October 6, 1990): 52.

[182] Image Credit: *http://up.botstudent.net/piltdown-man-new-york-times.jpg*

[183] Arthur Keith, *The Antiquity of Man* (London: Williams & Norgate, 1915).

[184] Arthur Keith, *The Antiquity of Man* (Philadelphia: J. B. Lippincott Company, 1928).

[185] National Science Foundation, *Evolution of Evolution: Flash Special Report Timeline:* *www.nsf.gov/news/special_reports/darwin/textonly/timeline.jsp* (September 2, 2015).

[186] Keith, 1915, p. 305.

[187] Volume I, *The Antiquity of Man* by Sir Arthur Keith. Philadelphia: J.B. Lippincott Company, 1925. Second Edition, Sixth Impression. Illustrated. Image Credit: *http://www.oakauctions.com/clarence-darrow-signed-%E2%80%9Cthe-antiquity-of-man%E2%80%9D-lot1674.aspx*.

[188] Isabelle De Groote, et al. "New genetic and morphological evidence suggests a single hoaxer created 'Piltdown man,'" *Royal Society Open Science*. 3 (2016).

[189] Image Credit: Wikipedia.

[190] William K. Gregory, "Hesperopithecus Apparently Not an Ape nor a Man," *Science*, 66 (1720) (December 16, 1927): 579–581.

[191] Ralph M. Wetzel, et al., "Catagonus, An 'Extinct' Peccary, Alive in Paraguay," *Science*, 189 (4200) (Aug. 1, 1975): 379.

[192] Duane T. Gish, *Evolution: The Fossils Still Say NO!* (El Cajon, CA: Institute for Creation Research, 1995). p. 328.

[193] Image Credit: This reconstruction of the La Chapelle-aux-Saints Neanderthal skeleton—discovered in France in 1908—was published in *L'Illustration* and in the *Illustrated London News* in 1909.

[194] Image Credit: Wikipedia.

[195] W.L. Jungers, "Lucy's length: Stature reconstruction in Australopithecus afarensis (A.L.288-1) with implications for other small-bodied hominids." *American Journal of Physical Anthropology.* 76 (2) (1988): 227–231.

[196] Some of these fatal flaws pertain to Lucy's actual fossil, some are in regards to how her fossil is represented, and some involve both.

[197] NOVA, *In Search of Human Origins (Part I)* (Airdate: June 3, 1997): *www.pbs.org/wgbh/nova/transcripts/2106hum1.html* (September 2, 2015).

[198] Time magazine reported in 1977 that Lucy had a tiny skull, a head like an ape, a braincase size the same as that of a chimp—450 cc. and "was surprisingly short legged" (*Time*, November 7, 1979, pp. 68–69). See also: Smithsonian National Museum of Natural History, "Australopithecus afarensis": *www.humanorigins.si.edu/evidence/human-fossils/species/australopithecus-afarensis* (September 2, 2015).

[199] Solly Zuckerman, *Beyond the Ivory Tower* (London: Taplinger Publishing Company, 1970), p. 78.

[200] Skull from: *www.skullsunlimited.com.*

[201] William H. Kimbel and Yoel Rak. "The Cranial Base of Australopithecus Afarensis: New Insights from the Female Skull." *Philosophical Transactions of the Royal Society B: Biological Sciences* 365.1556 (2010): 3365–3376.

[202] Upper Image Credit: M. H. Wolpoff, J. Hawks, B. Senut, M. Pickford, J. Ahern, "An Ape or the Ape: Is the Toumaï Cranium TM 266 a Hominid?" PaleoAnthropology. 2006: 36–50 (upper two images, arrows added). Lower Image Credit: Evolution Facts, Inc. *Evolution Encyclopedia Volume 2, Chapter 18 Ancient Man* (*www.godrules.net/evolutioncruncher/2evlch18a.htm*). (January 27, 2017). FM differences discussed in: William H. Kimbel and Rak Yoel. "The Cranial Base of Australopithecus Afarensis: New Insights from the Female Skull." *Philosophical Transactions of the Royal Society B: Biological Sciences* 365.1556 (2010): 3365–3376.

[203] Ibid., 3369–3370

[204] Image Credit: Wikipedia.

[205] Fred Spoor, Bernard Wood, Frans Zonneveld, "Implications of Early Hominid Labyrinthine Morphology for Evolution of Human Bipedal Locomotion," *Nature* 369 (June 23, 1994): 645–648.

[206] Smithsonian: *www.humanorigins.si.edu/evidence/human-fossils/species/australopithecus-africanus* (January 27, 2017).

[207] Bernard Wood, "A precious little bundle," *Nature* 443, 278–281 (September 21, 2006).

[208] Kate Wong, "Special Report: Lucy's Baby An extraordinary new human fossil comes to light," *Scientific American*: *www.scientificamerican.com/article/special-report-lucys-baby/* (September 20, 2006) (January 27, 2017).

[209] Healthline Bodymaps: *www.healthline.com/human-body-maps/semicircular-canals*. Medically Reviewed on January 26, 2015 by Healthline Medical Team (January 27, 2017).

[210] F. Spoor and F. Zonneveld. "Comparative review of the human bony labyrinth," *Am J Phys Anthropology*, Supplement 27 (1998): 211–51. P. Gunz, et al., "The Mammalian Bony Labyrinth Reconsidered: Introducing a Comprehensive Geometric Morphometric Approach," *Journal of Anatomy* 220, 6 (2012): 529–543.

[211] Fred Spoor, Bernard Wood, Frans Zonneveld, "Implications of Early Hominid Labyrinthine Morphology for Evolution of Human Bipedal Locomotion," *Nature* 369 (June 23, 1994): 645–648.

[212] Brian L. Day, et al. "The vestibular system," *Current Biology*, 15 (15), R583 - R586.

[213] Image Credit: Shutterstock.

[214] Adam Summers, "Born to Run: Humans will Never Win a Sprint against your Average Quadruped. But our Species is well-adapted for the Marathon," *Biomechanics*: *www.naturalhistorymag.com/biomechanics/112078/born-to-run* (September 1, 2015).

[215] Marc R. Meyer, Scott A. Williams, Michael P. Smith, Gary J. Sawyer, "Lucy's back: Reassessment of fossils associated with the A.L. 288-1 vertebral column," *Journal of Human Evolution*, 85 (August 2015): 174–180.

[216] Personal communication: "All [Lucy's bones were] found in an area covering about 3 square meters." Donald Johanson (May 28, 2014).

[217] *Atlas of Science*, "Archaeological surprise! Lucy has company," *https://atlasofscience.org/archaeological-surprise-lucy/* (November 30, 2015) (January 27, 2017).

[218] PBS Evolution, "Finding Lucy": *www.pbs.org/wgbh/evolution/library/07/1/l_071_01.html* (September 2, 2015).

[219] Ibid.

[220] F. Marchal, "A new morphometric analysis of the hominid pelvic bone," *Journal of Human Evolution*, 38(3) (March 2000): 347–65.

[221] Jack Stern & Randall L. Susman, "The Locomotor Anatomy of Australopithecus afarensis," *Journal of Physical Anthropology* 60 (1983): 291–292.

[222] Charles Oxnard, *The Order of Man: A Biomathematical Anatomy of the Primates* (Yale University Press and Hong Kong University Press, 1984): 3.

[223] Image Credit: *Australopithecus afarensis* (*History Alive! The Ancient World* (Palo Alto, CA: Teachers Curriculum Institute, 2004).

[224] Brian G. Richmond and David S. Strait, "Evidence That Humans Evolved From a Knuckle-Walking Ancestor," *Nature*, 404 (2000): 382–385.

[225] Maggie Fox, "Man's Early Ancestors Were Knuckle Walkers," *San Diego Union Tribune* (Quest Section, March 29, 2000).

[226] Richmond & Strait, *Evidence That Humans Evolved From a Knuckle-Walking Ancestor*, pp. 382–385.

[227] Guy Gugliotta, "It's All in the Wrist Early Human Ancestors Were 'Knuckle-Walkers,' Research Indicates," Washington Post (March 23, 2000), A03.

[228] Richmond & Strait, *Evidence That Humans Evolved From a Knuckle-Walking Ancestor*, pp. 382–385.

[229] Ibid.

[230] Manuel Domínguez-Rodrigo, Travis Rayne Pickering, Sergio Almécija, Jason L. Heaton, Enrique Baquedano, Audax Mabulla & David Uribelarrea, "Earliest modern human-like hand bone from a new >1.84-million-year-old site at Olduvai in Tanzania," *Nature Communications* 6, 7987 (2015); Jack Stern & Randall L. Susman, "The Locomotor Anatomy of Australopithecus afarensis," *Journal of Physical Anthropology* 60 (1983): 280.

[231] Ibid.

[232] Ibid.

[233] J. Stern & R. Susman, "The Locomotor Anatomy of Australopithecus afarensis," *Journal of Physical Anthropology* 60 (1983): 280.

[234] W. L. Jungers, "Lucy's limbs: skeletal allometry and locomotion in Australopithecus afarensis." *Nature* 297 (1982): 676–678.

[235] Stern & Susman, 1983.

[236] K.D. Hunt, "The evolution of human bipedality: ecology and functional morphology." *Journal of Human Evolution*, 26 (1994): 183–202.

[237] PBS Evolution, "Finding Lucy": *www.pbs.org/wgbh/evolution/library/07/1/l_071_01.html* (September 2, 2015); National Geographic, "What was 'Lucy'? Fast Facts on an Early Human Ancestor" (September 20, 2006). *National Geographic News: http://news.nationalgeographic.com/news/2006/09/060920-lucy.html* (September 2, 2015).

[238] Donald Johanson & Edgar Blake. *From Lucy to Language* (New York: Simon & Schuster, 1996).

[239] Image Credit: Answers in Genesis (left); Brian Thomas (right).

[240] Personal communication: "All [Lucy's bones were] found in an area covering about 3 square meters." Professor Donald Johanson (May 28, 2014).

[241] Licensed through Alamy. Photo Credit Franck Robichon/epa/Corbis.

[242] M. Häusler & P. Schmid, "Comparison of the Pelves of Sts 14 and AL 288-1: Implications for Birth and Sexual Dimorphism in Australopithecines." *Journal of Human Evolution* 29 (1995): 363–383.

[243] Alan Boyle, "Lucy or Brucey? It Can Be Tricky to Tell the Sex of Fossil Ancestors," *Science* (April 29, 2015).

[244] Image Credit: Wikipedia.

[245] Source: *http://news.utexas.edu/2016/08/29/ut-study-cracks-coldest-case-how-lucy-died* (January 27, 2017).

[246] J. Kappelman, R.A. Ketcham, S. Pearce, L. Todd, W. Akins, M.W. Colbert, et al, "Perimortem fractures in Lucy suggest mortality from fall out of tall tree." *Nature*, 537 (September 22, 2016): 503–507. *www.nature.com/nature/journal/v537/n7621/full/nature19332.html*

[247] Oxnard, *The Order of Man: A Biomathematical Anatomy of the Primates*, p. 3.

[248] Roger Lewin, *Bones of Contention* (Chicago: University of Chicago Press, 1987), p. 164.

[249] Wray Herbert, "Lucy's Uncommon Forbear," *Science News* 123 (February 5, 1983), p. 89.

[250] Albert W. Mehlert, "Lucy—Evolution's Solitary Claim for an Ape/Man: Her Position is Slipping Away," *Creation Research Society Quarterly*, 22 (3) (December, 1985), p. 145.

[251] Marvin Lubenow, *Bones of Contention* (Grand Rapids, MI: Baker Books, 1992), p. 179.

[252] DeWitt Steele & Gregory Parker, *Science of the Physical Creation*, 2d ed. (Pensacola, FL: A Beka Book, 1996), p. 299.

[253] "Before humans left Babel, it appears that apes had already spread over much of the Old World and had diversified into a large array of species… Paleontologists are still discovering species of post-Flood apes. If we are correct about post-Flood rocks, apes were at their highest point of diversity and were buried in local catastrophes just before humans spread out from Babel." Kurt Wise, "Lucy Was Buried First Babel Helps Explain the Sequence of Ape and Human Fossils," (August 20, 2008), *Answers in Genesis: www.answersingenesis.org/human-evolution/lucy/lucy-was-buried-first/* (September 2, 2015).

[254] Hugh Ross, "Species Development: Natural Process or Divine Action," Creation and Time Audiotape, Tape 2, Side 1 (Pasadena, CA: Reasons to Believe, 1990).

[255] World Wide Fund For Nature, "What do Pandas eat? The simple answers is: bamboo," Pando.org: *www.wwf.panda.org/what_we_do/endangered_species/giant_panda/panda/what_do_pandas_they_eat/* (February 13, 2017).

[256] Nathaniel T. Jeanson, "Did Lions Roam the Garden of Eden?" ICR.org: *www.icr.org/article/did-lions-roam-garden-eden/* (February 13, 2017).

[257] Overview Eric Hovind and Paul Taylor welcome special guest Dr. G. Charles Jackson in the August 18, 2011 episode of Creation Today.

[258] John MacArthur, "Creation: Believe It or Not, Part 2 (90–209)": *www.gty.org/resources/sermons/90-209/creation-believe-it-or-not-part-2* (March 28, 1999) (January 27, 2017).

[259] Ham, Ken. "Culture and Church in Crisis." *AnswersinGenesis.com*: *www.answersingenesis.org/articles/am/v2/n1/culture-church-crisis.* Accessed January 1, 2014. Survey data: *www.answersingenesis.org/articles/am/v2/n1/aig-poll (data).* Accessed January 1, 2014.

[260] Summarized from: Southern Baptist Convention. "How to Become a Christian." *www.sbc.net/knowjesus/theplan.asp.* Accessed March 16, 2016.